Love Later On

Love Later On

Peggy Knickerbocker

Illustrations
by
Karen Barbour

gatekeeper press™

ALSO BY PEGGY KNICKERBOCKER

Olive Oil: From Tree to Table

The Rose Pistola Cookbook
with Reed Hearon

Simple Soirees
Seasonal Menus for Sensational Dinner Parties

The San Francisco Ferry Plaza Farmers' Market Cookbook
with Christopher Hirsheimer

For Robert

Cover & Book designed by
Christopher Hirsheimer, Canal House

Published by Gatekeeper Press
2167 Stringtown Rd, Suite 109
Columbus, OH 43123-2989
GatekeeperPress.com

First Edition: May, 2021

Library of Congress Control Number 2021936548

ISBN 9781662911675

Chapter One

B Y THE TIME I BOUGHT MY HOUSE on Russian Hill after forty years of an intermittent single life, I was sixty. Despite a few new aches and pains, I fully expected the approaching decade to be my best. Mind, body, and soul, I'd never been in better shape. Since I didn't think of myself as a senior, what got to me were the checkers at the market asking if I needed help to my car or well-meaning people who offered me seats on the bus. With hair that was still blondish, an athletic vitality, and a good-humored attitude, I felt more like forty-two.

Once again, I was a woman without a man. But my acceptance of this state—my joy in the peace and simple pleasures of living alone—were new for me. Each morning when I pulled back the curtains in my bedroom, I could see

San Francisco Bay stretching before me with ships gliding in and out of the Golden Gate, while my two snowy ragdoll cats purred in the warm white folds of my covers.

In 1896 my gray wooden row house had been built for a sea captain. During the fifteen years I'd rented it, it had been the scene of considerable fun, a couple of failed attempts at romance, and a lot of deferred maintenance. When it went on the market after I had just extricated myself from a disastrous four-year relationship, I pounced. I planned to live in it alone rather than sharing my life with another man who didn't stack up.

Now that I owned my house, I made it fully mine, doing everything I'd dreamed about, making it a welcoming place for the friends and house guests who filled my life. The living room, just off my little back garden had been lacquered red for years, just like my mother's. I painted it a more subtle color--a sophisticated grayish brown that warmed up at night in the light that glowed from the fireplace and candles and lamps with mica shades. With my bookcases completely filled, I stacked the overflowing books everywhere, with vases of flowers and little treasures perched on top of them.

With the aid of my stylish opinionated friend Randal

Breski, who has an unerring eye and who, like me, had lived and shopped in Paris, I chose fabrics and paints for the rest of the house. We made the dining room feel French with pale green walls and taffeta curtains. On summer evenings, a low gold light streamed across the old hardwood floors and my mother's mahogany dining table that could seat up to eighteen. Winter dinners were candlelit.

My dinners were more casual and fun than my mother's. Hers tended to be boozy, heavy, and creamy. Mine were easy going and lighter, with fish or good red meat, lots of vegetables, salads, and fruit. While I served my guests wine, I no longer drank it myself, having given up alcohol when I was forty, after nearly letting it wreck my life. I cooked with ingredients my mother had never used—fennel, radicchio, hunks of aged cheeses, and essentials like good extra virgin olive oil and varied vinegars. She'd resorted to shortcuts out of a can or the freezer; I made food from scratch. Men wore neckties to her dinners and her guests didn't include writers, teachers, blacksmiths, artists, gay men, and women, or chefs, but she did invite Alan Watts and Dianne Feinstein along with other political types and theater people.

As a renter, I had cooked in my fifty-year-old kitchen,

testing recipes for several cookbooks I'd written and for dinner parties. It was beyond ready for a renovation and definitely needed more than the one heavily over-loaded electrical outlet. With the help of an architect friend, the room was transformed. We kept the black and white tile floor, and brought the electricity up to code, adding a commercial stove, a farmhouse kitchen sink, and marble counters. A glass chandelier provided a certain sparkle. At last, the room that was the center of my life and my work as a food writer was ideal for me and the food-loving friends who cooked there with me. I'd met many of them in the late 1990s when I started writing about food for Saveur Magazine, and other publications. They were my people. But others went all the way back—I'd known two of my closest friends Cal Ferris and Flicka McGurrin since we were seven-year-olds. With Flicka, I'd opened a restaurant in North Beach in the 1970s and another one on the waterfront in the '80s. And alongside, we ran a cooking school and a catering business. When we started, we had no experience with business or cooking for more than 6 to 8 people, but we cooked what we loved and they sent back empty plates.

Another of my dearest friends had been the first to

call my attention to my "heightened domestic urges." The novelist Armistead Maupin had been introduced to my domesticity during the early days of my first and only marriage. He'd gone to college with my ex-husband Jay Hanan and later came out as a gay rights leader. Armistead and I had spent hours talking about men, straight and gay, but for a long time, neither of us had been terribly lucky in love.

Tending to act upon my urges more swiftly than was wise, I'd repeatedly found myself with a man far too soon, since I had trouble being alone in a sea of couples-sometimes. My lapses in judgment had chipped away at my self-esteem. I'd fall into a swoon, get into a romance and wake up a few years later wondering what hit me. The men I was consistently attracted to were roguish and immature, the more off-beat the better. I began to think I should hire a private eye before getting into something deep one more time. But what was the definition of a good man anyway? And what kind of good man would be the right one for me? Why had I been afraid to aim high, when I'd always aimed high in my career and choice of friends.

Now that I was single, I expected my house to be my

sanctuary. My walled garden had become the jewel of the first floor. The mirror that had been placed on its center wall, surrounded by an arch of ivy, cleverly reflected a painting through the glass doors in the living room. The tiny trimmed green space gave the impression of being another room. And the white flowers I'd planted around the edges to catch the light of the moon appeared to be floating in the garden at night. It was all very romantic but I was certain there would be no more love affairs. Just me, my kitties and my friends.

I planned to keep sleeping alone in my bedroom. Because of its view across the bay and its amazing light, I felt it was the best room in the house. It was there that I spent most of my time—reading, talking on the phone, and on my laptop. Across the hall, I freshened up my writing room by painting it forest green; its new orange shelves held 400 cookbooks. But I kept my one small old-fashioned bathroom just as it was and deliberately didn't put in a shower (the lack of one had been a source of complaints from men.) The claw-legged bathtub was fine for me.

By the time I was sixty-three in 2008, I considered the existence I'd worked out for myself to be rich and overflowing. At least 85 percent of the time I was good with being single. I was alone but not often lonely. Still, there was that missing percentage. And so when my lifelong friend Cal Ferris called to tell me about a dinner conversation she'd had the night before, I pricked up my ears.

Cal had invited over Steve and Nan Grand-Jean, a couple I also knew and as the evening was winding down, Steve mentioned a dear pal who'd recently lost his wife of 44 years. His name was Robert Fisher. He was such a great guy, they told her. In fact, they went on about him—his solid honest character, his tender and emotional state. They also said he was very funny. They couldn't bear to see him in pain. He'd stopped working to take care of his wife for the four or five years her illness lingered. "Who could we introduce him to?" they asked over dessert. Cal and her husband Tim Ferris responded at the same time, "What about Peggy Knickerbocker?"

Chapter Two

A FEW DAYS LATER, I WONDERED WHY I had the urge to wander into the lingerie department of Bloomingdale's. I had just seen a film with my closest movie friend, Terry Gamble, as we did most Friday afternoons. She went off to spend the weekend with her family and left me asking myself, *Did I really need anything new?* If so, what was I doing in the lacy section where I always went when there was a glimmer of someone on the horizon.

It must have had something to do with the conversation I'd had with Cal about the guy who had recently lost his wife. I'd wanted to know just how great this guy was. And Cal told me exactly what I wanted to hear about Robert Fisher's solid character, his gentle inquisitive nature, and how wonderful he'd been to his wife. She went on to say he was very interested in food. But then, who wasn't?

"How odd to hear about him now," I told her, "when I've been congratulating myself for coming to grips with being alone." I'd assured Cal that my longings to have a mate had dwindled. But of course, these are the moments we'd better pay attention to, the moments when all is good, but in fact, something even better is around the bend.

So there I was in the lingerie department on the first day of a very long winter weekend. I mention the extent of the weekend, since weekends alone at any time of year had a way of getting me down; me, and many other single women. A saleswoman appeared. We made a few choices and she led me into a dressing room. There, in front of the all-too- truthful triptych mirrors and harsh lights, I felt wary. Before thinking about getting to know this man, this Robert Fisher, I flashed to getting undressed in front of him. It's not easy in middle age. And who was I kidding, was I still even in middle age at 63?

As I climbed into bed that night, my thoughts again turned to Robert Fisher. I supposed I wanted to meet him, but I dreaded those odious first dates. The idea of getting all done up in tights and Spanx was off-putting, and opening the front door and sizing up the poor guy would be even worse. In my imagination, we would suffer through a mediocre meal at a restaurant of his choosing, where it would be so loud we couldn't hear each other speak. Then he'd take me home, wouldn't kiss me because that's the rule on a first date, and even though I didn't really like him, I'd feel rejected when he didn't call.

Still, here I was thinking about this available man, when only days before I was convinced that I was fine on my own. The residue of my most recent failed romance was behind me. I was game for taking another crack, but this time, I told myself sternly, it would have to be a better-informed one.

A few weeks passed without a peep from Robert Fisher. I felt a little embarrassed that I'd talked about him all over town. He couldn't have any idea what the mere possibility of a meeting a good man could do to a woman with a record like mine.

Then one day I ran into Nan Grand-Jean in front of a café in North Beach. She told me about a list Robert had made of the attributes for his ideal woman. A friend had suggested that he do this. The act of writing it had made him feel better, so he sent it to this friend, who was CEO of a company, asking jokingly that it be shown to the director of the human resources department. Nan and Steve had been sent a copy, too, but I didn't want to be pushy and ask to see it. I told Nan I didn't know what to think about this list-making and that I'd never dated businessmen anyway. "And how has that worked out for you, Peggy?" she asked.

One Saturday morning not long after that, I returned from an early trip to the Ferry Plaza Farmers' Market where I go every week, to shop for vegetables, flowers, and fruit. I unpacked my produce and settled down with a nice frothy cappuccino to check my emails.

An email from Robert Fisher. I shrieked before opening it. "Oh God," I said aloud. I got fluttery. There had been no warning. I wished I had at least seen a picture of him.

In his email, so raw it was jarring, he said he was an amateur when it came to meeting women: he had been married to his late wife for 44 years. He didn't know the rules or how to proceed. But he was coming to San Francisco and wanted to take me out to dinner. Or, would I prefer coffee? Then he said he'd call me a little later in the day, when he returned home from watching his grandsons play basketball. He lived in Los Angeles. He'd been up all night perusing my website.

That email was telling. He seemed loyal and humble. He admitted he was new at dating, so I assumed he hadn't fooled around as a husband. It sounded as if he'd never even gone out on a date.

I liked hearing that he spent time with his grandchildren. And how could I help but be comforted by the fact that he'd been with the same woman all his life?

Oh, God. Heart be still. I should have been able to take this in stride, been steady and sure of myself like Deborah Kerr in the movie I'd watched the night before, *The Beloved Infidel*. She'd worn a tight emerald green dress with a girdle, a pointy bra, and gloves. She'd crossed her legs with exaggerated femininity as she flirted with F. Scott Fitzgerald, reeling him in with ease. I couldn't flirt if I tried.

I thought of my father's situation while my mother was lingering in a near-vegetative state for a few painful years after having a stroke at the age of fifty-seven. In those last years, a great friend of my parents' named Marti Fletcher had come from her family ranch in Sonoma once a week to read to my mother. Of all their friends, Marti was my favorite. She had been a communist at one point and lived in France on and off for seventeen years.

When she returned to California for vacations, she'd take me riding, my favorite thing to do as a horse-crazed kid. Marti never talked down to Tony, my younger brother, or me and always asked the best questions—what I liked to read and what did I think about our president. She was gutsy, smart, and told the truth.

A few months after our mothers' funeral, Tony and I urged our father to take Marti to the theater. My father had been the film and drama critic for the San Francisco Chronicle for years. Our mother had suffered for three or four years after a stroke, and when there was no change in her condition, she'd effectively stopped eating. Her illness and death had been terribly difficult for our dad, and there was absolutely no reason his life shouldn't improve.

When I asked my father, a few weeks after our suggestion, if he'd called Marti, he stalled and looked uncharacteristically reticent. He said he worried that she might reject him. "The fear of rejection at sixty-three?" I exclaimed in disbelief. I was in my early thirties, single, and living with a daily fear of rejection after various missteps. "Jesus, get a grip," I remember saying, half joking. Now, I was sixty-three, and I realized that I was just as hesitant as my father had been at the same age. With Robert's phone call impending, I was feeling vulnerable.

As I waited to hear from him, I puttered in my newly remodeled kitchen, where I was still rearranging dishes and sorting things out. I thought about having lunch with Robert Fisher at the little marble table I'd just bought, and sitting with him in the Philippe Stark ghost chairs that went alongside. Struck by a sudden culinary urge, I soaked some white beans in water to cook later with a bay leaf, a Parmesan rind, and a splash of olive oil. I couldn't relax; I was restless.

I jumped when the phone rang, but the call was from Pam Hunter, whom I'd known mostly from my years as a food writer, "I hope you are calling," I said, " because you've discovered that the amazing gray flannel coat you wore last week to the restaurant opening is too big for you, and you want to offer it to me."

But no, that was not the reason. Pam had just talked to Robert! She'd known him for years. He had asked her to put in a good word. "Robert is a seriously good man," she said, and added that he was smart and funny and honest", everything you'd want in a man".

We hung up, and I waited another half hour. Still no Robert. So, I called Steve Grand-Jean. He thought Bob, as he called him, and I would have a lot in common, especially concerning our mutual favorite subject—food. Being in the investment world, Bob was well-versed in the financial side of the food world, and intuitive about knowing which concepts would be a hit, early on. He had been enthusiastic about Starbucks and Il Fornaio, for instance. If he walked into a shopping mall, he'd know exactly what sort of brand would thrive there. Steve made a point of telling me that in high school in St. Louis, Bob had been a terrific athlete--a star in baseball, football, and basketball. That was such a masculine way of evaluating someone, I thought. A woman would probably not have mentioned that.

I put my beans on to simmer and started braising some lamb shanks. Maybe I'd invite some friends over tonight or the next. I made a salad with lovely pale pink radicchio leaves that were marbled like endpapers on a book. Into it went some good Rogue River blue cheese and sliced beets that I'd roasted earlier.

As I finished my salad, the phone rang. My mouth was still full and I was chewing. I choked and sputtered and coughed, trying to swallow. The kitties meowed for attention, a cable car clanked by. Everything happened at once. I needed a glass of water. That didn't go down well either.

"Are you all right?" Robert asked. "Did I get you at a bad time?"

"No, no," I assured him. Still gasping, I said, "I was just finishing lunch. I've been looking forward to your call. How was the basketball game?"

And so we gave it our best shot. I asked about what he liked to be called, as I'd heard him referred to as "Bob," yet he'd signed his email "Robert." He told me that his old friends and people from St. Louis called him Bob; so had his late wife, Bonnie. He told me to call him anything I liked. So I decided I'd call him Robert.

And then, before we'd covered any ground, I heard a loud snoring sound. *Really* loud. "Am I boring you already?" I asked.

"Oh no, that's my bulldog," he told me. "That's Darlin'. Or it could be Baby, the French bulldog. They lie down; they start to snore. They even snore with their eyes open."

I found myself wondering, a little ahead of myself, how his dogs would get along with my cats. "Two dogs?" I asked. "I have two cats, Ragdolls, Lola and Lucie."

"Well, actually,'" he said, "I have two other dogs:

Lily—a petit basset griffon vendeen—and Cosmo, an old wire-haired dachshund. They are just quieter. I don't know what I'd do without them right now."

"That's a coincidence," I said, grasping at something that would link us. "I grew up with dachshunds. One of them was called Harris Tweed, a wire-haired. And we had a black, smooth-haired dachshund called Robin, a barker and a nipper. But my father grew up with English bulldogs." Then I added that I had recently fallen in love with petit basset griffons.

Animals are always a good way to get started, but then…What else could we talk about?

Silence.

Dead silence.

I am an animated woman. Some might say overly so. My laugh is loud and I am excitable, a bit of a gusher, though never an inauthentic one. I look for the good in everyone, at least at first. I don't pass on unkind information about my friends. I can keep a secret. I have been told that while I think I am tough, I really have a big, soft heart. All that may be true, but when a conversation is going nowhere, I don't endure silences comfortably. So pretty soon I'd either have to come up with a new subject or get off the phone.

I told Robert I was sorry about the death of his wife, and he told me it was hard and he wasn't adjusting well. "I can't imagine how hard it must be," I said.

Another silence.

Then we agreed we felt awkward on the phone and that maybe emailing would be easier.

I asked him if he'd send me his list of what he was looking for in a woman.

When I put down the receiver, I felt the shiver of an old familiar melancholy settling in. When it came to men, that melancholy was never far from me, just waiting for a chance to descend and coalesce into a defeatist feeling. It was a sense of futility I had allowed to shadow me for many years. And it was boring the hell out of me. This time, however, a faint spark of energy urged me on. Plus I had nothing to lose except what I'd built up in my mind.

So I suppressed the melancholy and did what I often do on Saturday afternoons at home: I gathered my reading material and laptop and flopped down on my bed. The view from my window changes daily, hourly—it's moody and breathtaking to me, even after fifteen years of living in the house. The Golden Gate Bridge, off to the west, is more brick-colored than golden. It can be totally obscured by fog during the day. And at night when it's foggy, the faint lights of its towers provide the only hint that it is there at all.

That afternoon, the Bay was struck by a feeble February sun, as huge cargo ships inched in under the bridge, accompanied by little tugboats to guide them to port. Sailboats glided by, hoping to catch a breeze. I lay on my bed watching the light fade, not feeling as satisfied as I wanted to be.

I have to say that I have never been fond of Saturday evenings at home alone. Armistead Maupin had once asked why solitary Saturday nights bothered me so much. "You are a writer; you can work on a Saturday night." While Amistead usually understood me pretty well, here, he missed the point. Whenever I found myself alone like this, I always wondered whether everyone in the world was out kicking up her heels except me. What I honestly longed for most was to have the right man by my side, someone with whom I could watch a movie, read a book, or just eat a good dinner. Lacking that man, I had to do what I could to feel secure. As the late afternoon was fading, I had to admit that nothing was working.

I was still feeling unsettled about the call. I didn't know whether to go downstairs and make a cup of chamomile tea or a double espresso.

CHAPTER THREE

W HERE DO WE BEGIN TELLING each other about our past six decades, was Robert's first message to me. Now that we had to start accounting for those years, the prospect must have seemed as overwhelming to him as it did to me.

"*I have a million questions.*" I wrote back. But then something prompted me to take the plunge. For me, Bonnie was the big unknown. I knew it would be unwise if I avoided talking about her.

"*For starters, I'd love to hear about Bonnie, how you and she met*"?

For a half-hour or so there was not a word from him. Had I hit a nerve, made him pull back before we barely got started? But when Robert finally wrote back, he sounded happy to be immersed in his earliest memories of Bonnie, drawn back to the hot summer afternoon at a

St. Louis swimming pool when he couldn't take his eyes off a lean, graceful girl who was approaching the diving board. He was only a boy of twelve, but it was love at first sight. *"I felt certain she was the most beautiful girl I'd ever seen."* By the time Bonnie dived into the pool, he knew he would marry her. And he did, eight years later, when both of them were twenty.

That first memory of Bonnie never faded. I wondered if he was ready to be thinking about another woman. I admit that I also fixated on *graceful* and *lean,* words that had never been part of my description, though I'd always gotten compliments on my legs.

When I asked Robert whether he considered his long marriage successful, he said, *"It was one of the world's great marriages. It wasn't always perfect, but we never bickered or really argued. Of course, we had some differences of opinion, particularly on child-raising."* He'd thought Bonnie was too lenient with the kids and didn't feel they should be shielded from him when he came home from work, spent, and cranky. Like me, Bonnie had been influenced by the permissive attitudes of the Sixties and Seventies.

What was that time like in St. Louis? I wondered. Apparently, his wife had been a serious, spirited, socially conscious young woman who wore Birkenstocks and taught dance to inner-city children, but her ideas about the role of a wife seemed to come straight out of the Fifties. For Bonnie, Robert told me, the man came first. She'd tended to let him have his way, but she also quietly and adeptly managed to do as she saw fit.

I let him know that my ex-husband Jay and I had been on equal ground, I'd never done much maneuvering because I didn't know how to fool him into thinking he'd made a decision.

It helped that the Fishers had been madly in love. The two of them had grown up together with an appreciation of many of the same things. Robert had encouraged Bonnie's involvement with the dance world. After performances, there'd been parties for visiting dance companies at their house in St. Louis. Then, when they moved to Los Angeles in the mid-80s, the two of them became excited about the work of a group of Southern California artists and started to collect their paintings. Since I knew some of those artists and their work, I definitely wanted to hear more about this—but not then. So, I steered Robert back to writing about what had made their marriage click. One of the secrets of their success seemed to be that they'd always set aside plenty of time for themselves, even though they adored their three children.

As I learned more about this woman, I began asking myself what qualities of hers I possessed and wondering whether Robert would really be open to an entirely different kind of woman. My Sixties and Seventies outfits had never included Birkenstocks. From the little Robert told me, I tried to get a picture of what Bonnie was really like. But I felt no need to compete with her. By this time in my life, I was able to hear about this accomplished woman with interest. Besides, I had no skin in the game, yet. There was something touching about Robert's openness—his eagerness to share his memories of his wife and first love as if it had never occurred to him that anything he told me could possibly make me feel jealous. It was as if there was trust between us already.

Before I knew anything about Bonnie, I'd imagined her just as a wife and mother. But the work she did as a dance teacher had been important to her. Robert proudly called her "*a humanitarian, always taking on causes for the underdog.*" I was fascinated to hear that she'd gotten a degree in psychotherapy and had specialized in working with schizophrenics.

"*Take your meds!*" she'd call out the car window if she saw one of her patients shambling down the street in LA. I'd thought of her as tall, but Robert said she was petite -- "*Tiny, five feet four, with beautiful long curly hair and she was as irreverent as a sailor.*"

"*Irreverent as a sailor?*" I felt we would have gotten along, become friends if we'd known each other.

When I asked about his kids, he was eager to tell me about them. All three of them had followed in the footsteps of their parents and married early. His son Cass, the youngest and the intellectual of the family, was a professor of Religious Studies who lived in Florida with his wife, Mariana from Prague. His daughters, Jackie and Carrie, both in their forties, lived in Los Angeles and had kids of their own.

They'd all been hit very hard by their mother's death; their heads were still spinning. I thought about how recent it had been, how loyal the three of them must feel to the memory of their mother, how unthinkable they might find it that another woman could ever step in as their father's squeeze. But just as I was worrying about all this, Robert said something that I found surprising, given that this was only our first day of communication. *"I hope you'll meet them one day, I'm so proud of them."*

I couldn't help wishing I had some kids to talk about. I knew how much I'd missed by not having my own family, but at least I'd lived with a couple of wonderful children. When I was with the artist Ed Handelman in the early '70s, his daughter Ana lived with us full time. I loved being part of a little family and doing things with her. When I took her to get her ears pierced, she was fine; I fainted. And I took her shopping to the same stores my mother had taken me. When I brought her to meet my parents, what fascinated her most about their flat was not their spectacular view, but the fact that they had a home bar with a silver ice bucket and silver tongs like the ones used by characters on TV. Our outings made a lasting bond between us; Ana has never forgotten to send me a message for my birthday or Mother's Day.

My unfortunate last boyfriend, at least, had an adorable little girl—Madeleine. Getting to know her was the best thing—and the only good thing —to come out of that relationship. Like Ana, Madeline and I are close and she visits when she's in town.

"I have a minute family", I wrote Robert, *just seven of*

us. I am close to Tony, my only sibling, his second wife Mary, and his three grown kids. Things weren't always as warm during his first marriage because the rapport between his ex-wife and me was strained. I was a big, bossy older sister and a bit of an Auntie Mame to his kids. I've mellowed now and Tony and I speak almost daily about our family, what we're cooking or what's coming up in his garden. And we all spend lots of time together including hikes, birthdays and holidays."

I wanted to give Robert a sense of my very congenial single life, but I found myself feeling defensive after all this talk about marriage and kids. So, instead of beginning in a positive way, I wrote, *"Invariably, when I go to a nail salon,"* I wrote, *"a nice manicurist would, as she began to work on my hands, tilt her head, tap my empty ring finger and ask with phony compassion, Not married?"*

"I always want to say, No, I'm not married, and I'm just fine thank you."

I also told Robert that I felt at a loss whenever an invitation to a wedding arrived addressed to Peggy Knickerbocker and guest. It wasn't easy to go to weddings alone, but I could never think of anyone to bring. *"Luckily little attention is paid to traditional seating arrangements these days. The orientations of my friends are all over the map anyway. I'm always happy to sit next to women of any persuasion, gay men, or interesting straight men."*

I wanted Robert to understand that in some unexpected ways, it wasn't always easy to be single, but that most of the time, I actually felt pretty good about being on my own.

"I probably wouldn't have traveled as much if I'd been part of a family. I might not have formed some of my warmest friendships or been able to dedicate myself to my various careers. I know I wouldn't have had the unforgettable time I did during the five years I had an apartment in Paris."

I was making a strong case for why I didn't need him, and once I'd hit the send button, I felt ridiculous. He wrote back confessing that because he and Bonnie didn't have many single women friends, he'd never given much thought to the lives of unattached women. They'd hung out mostly with business friends or other couples and their own children. *"But,"* he added, as if he was trying to change to a safer subject," *I've been to Paris on business and with Bonnie. I'm intrigued to hear about your apartment and life there."*

"That makes me a little sad, I replied. *My friendships with married couples are positively vital. I've always been accepted for who I am. And in fact, when I brought along someone like the last boyfriend, I would have been more appreciated unaccompanied. I like*

— 40 —

to think I was good fun to be around and I hope my friends, married or otherwise, found me interesting and game. I guess I provided a buffer for some couples".

By then it was time for dinner, so instead of going further into this discussion, we decided to pick up where we left off the next morning. I could have gone on, but I was grateful for the time to stand back, evaluate how our emailing each other was going. I had the urge to call my close friends and tell them what was happening. But instead of acting like an eighth-grader, I acted my age, although I did have a kind of eighth-grade flutter in my heart. A sense of excitement and doubt raced around in my brain. I had no interest in dinner at all. I found it hard to concentrate, to read. I couldn't wait to see what would happen next. The thought of going to Paris together entered my mind and then I made myself lower my expectations.

But wouldn't you know—instead of Robert waiting until morning, it was around 9:00 pm when he wrote to say he'd just returned from dinner with neighbors. *I spent the whole evening talking about you.* I was elated, and a bit relieved. Apparently, apart from the time it took to write to each other, the emailing was going well for both of us.

He wrote that when he got home, he'd reread some of my articles, feeling that now he knew me better. And he said that he was curious about my last boyfriend, whom he pointed out I'd mentioned a couple of times.

I felt it was too soon to go into it. As I wrote back saying we could discuss my love life at a later point, another email from Robert crossed mine. I could tell he'd been doing a lot of research on me. This time he brought up the piece I'd published in *Saveur* about my mothers' red dining room, an article that happened to be a favorite of mine.

Christopher Hirsheimer, co-founder of the magazine *Saveur* had asked me to write it. Always giving me a chance to write pieces that really mattered to me, she had changed my writing career by her enthusiasm for my ideas, and we'd become great friends along the way. The piece was a sentimental reflection about my mother's Mississippi roots and her cornbread stuffing with bacon drippings. I'd described how I'd adapted her traditional recipe for the Thanksgiving meals I served in my own red dining room. Robert had also been moved by my piece on North Beach, the cover story for the first issue of *Saveur* in 1994. That article had given him a sense of my life after the end of my first marriage in a lusty, boozy artistic neighborhood, close to the house I was living in now.

Your life is beginning to seem like a movie, he wrote me, *Very cinematic. And I don't mean to pry, but you've mentioned Christopher Hirsheimer quite intentionally, are you very close to him?*

I explained that Christopher was a woman who had grown up with four brothers and that her mother had always liked the name. She was a beautiful, tall blond with the best sense of humor in the world.

He told me he was relieved to hear this. He said he'd felt a streak of jealousy rush through him and he thought he should ask.

Although it seemed a little soon for him to feel like this, his allusion to jealousy didn't trouble me at all. In fact, I was having such a good time writing him, I didn't mind that I was home alone this particular Saturday night. Robert was 'full of beans,' as my mother used to say about someone enthusiastic and energetic. And this was new in my experience—a man actually being eager and available. Most men I'd met were evasive and withholding. God forbid, you might think they were interested in you.

I was charmed by his guilelessness: *"You're not at all like some of the women who've dropped off chicken soup or mailed me CD's since Bonnie died"*

"No casseroles yet?" I shot back.

I now felt comfortable enough to ask him when he was going to send me the list I'd been hearing about. *"Don't worry, I won't take it terribly seriously. I'm hardly a cookie-cutter woman".*

He sent it attached to the next email, admitting he was feeling self-conscious and saying I could just read the thing and not think it was the basis of any sort of audition. He called it a lighthearted exercise--a way to escape from his gloom. Apart from me, it had only been sent to Steve and Nan Grand-Jean and his favorite CEO.

My Ideal Woman
January 2008

1. I will instantly be crazy about her........head over heels in love
2. I will learn from her-----she will make me a better and more complete person
3. She will have a healthy self-esteem......she will not be afraid of Bonnie's spirit...she will embrace her memory
4. She's got to be smart
5. She will be independent...a success on her own.... low maintenance

6. She will have a contagious sense of humor....quick to laugh

7. She will be totally feminine ..... elegant, bewitching, graceful

8. She will be between 45–54 years old

9. If she is white .... she will have blond, shoulder-length hair

10. It's fine if she is Black or Brown or anything else

11. She will be uninhibited

12. She will be a good dancer.... she's got to have rhythm

13. She will be incredibly interesting...able to talk on any subject.... be a fascinating dinner partner.......hosts and hostesses will want her next to them

14. She will be coyly shy...Audrey Hepburnesque.....

15. She will be up for anything ...spending her life with me, she'll need to be......she will be thrilled by not knowing what tomorrow brings....she will be able to ride a rocket ship with no stirrups... she will hold on because she has strong knees and the will to hang on...never letting go!

16. She will be a romantic but have better judgment than I.....she will be more tethered to reality

17. She will be a Democrat

I remember thinking, he sure used a lot of dots. But that was my way of not facing what his list really meant. I tend to seize upon the superficial so that I do not have to go too deep when I get uncomfortable. Nevertheless, his move had been optimistic. In fact, his list reminded me of an old self-help book I'd read about "putting one's wishes out in the universe." Now that I'd read it, I didn't feel the least bit intimidated. In fact, except for my age and my complete lack of any resemblance to Audrey Hepburn, I felt that I could be a good choice. But, many of my women friends would also have filled the bill. I thought the rocket ship reference was a little full of itself. And as to my self-esteem, he'd find out soon enough that it was a work in progress. When he wanted his woman to be 'uninhibited', I was sure he'd meant being uninhibited about sex. That would depend upon our chemistry, I thought, which at this point was the big unknown, but the entire list did have an earthy, playful quality, which seemed promising, dots and all.

"You know I'm 63," I wrote him, feeling the need to put that card on the table.

Steve Grand-Jean had already told him that and he didn't seem to care. He knew by looking at my pictures and reading my articles that he was interested.

He must have been reading my mind. Now I wondered what this guy looked like. I didn't want to sound shallow, but I asked if he had a photograph to send. He promised to look for one. I explained that I too had Googled him but hadn't come up with a thing.

Who was this man without a past? I told him I'd even wondered if he was CIA or FBI. Robert explained that since he'd been taking care of Bonnie for the past five years, he'd had to stop working and had been totally out of circulation.

"I've worked all my life in securities, before there was a Google, want me to send you my CV?"

"No thanks, just a photograph, please."

"Okay, but in case you are worried," he said, *"I'm not a dog."*

Chapter Four

B Y THE TIME WE TOLD EACH OTHER good night, I realized I was too excited to read or even sleep. The deep breaths I took to calm myself only reinvigorated me. As I tossed and turned, I reviewed everything that happened over the course of our brief correspondence. I loved that he'd said he wasn't a dog. For a businessman, that was pretty cool, and thank God, he had a sense of humor. He must have been good at being a husband and father—so different from anyone I'd gone for in the past forty years.

Why had men like him never before attracted me? Because I didn't think they would go for me, I'd always made excuses that they would have been too square. Instead, I'd gone for men who reflected my own restlessness and need to rebel, men who represented novelty and challenge.

Well, I'd thought of them as men, but most of them didn't measure up. Perhaps I'd needed to feel superior to them in order to boost my morale—a typical pattern for people who drink too much.

They'd all had an edge that initially attracted me, an edge that blinded me even in my sober mid-forties when I chose to waste my time with a charming junkie. He was clean when we met, but lost his appeal once he slipped back into his old ways. I went to Narcotics Anonymous meetings with him (his particular group was called *Fuck No*) where I was the only woman in the room who wasn't tattooed, riddled with piercings, or a pole dancer. Back then, I honestly didn't know why I was drawn to him, but later I understood. When I first got sober, I couldn't imagine having sex without some substance to lower my inhibitions. With him sex was easy. He was sweet and kind and had that seductive junkie allure that everyone in NA knew only too well. He even folded my laundry and watered my garden. He was also twelve years younger—I suppose that was attractive to a woman of forty-five.

Having sex sober was all-new to me. It was raw and real. I could feel everything. It grabbed my heart and fogged my brain.

Of course, I imagined I could change him. The truth was, I was not only ashamed to be with an addict, I was also mortified that he probably hadn't read a book since sixth grade. I thought I'd be able to keep the affair going as I worked on his transformation, but of course, the whole thing fell apart because we had nothing in common. When I met his mother, she asked me what a lovely woman was doing with her sad sack of a son. (I couldn't tell her it was the sex.)

After we broke up, I had more therapy, went to all sorts of meetings, and promised myself I'd never again go for a man who wasn't up to me. But about seven years later, a dashing French lawyer broke a long spell of undesired celibacy. I met him at a Christmas dinner in Paris in the late '90s. After dinner at a mutual friend's house, he took me salsa dancing and back to his apartment where we sat gazing out of his window at a sparkling Eiffel Tower. He told me funny stories in French and drank whisky, a lot. I don't think he noticed that I was stone-cold sober. I was smitten by the romance of the situation that allowed me to overlook the flaws. This Frenchman was difficult as well as charming, but his non-negotiable flaw proved to be the drinking. (I won't call it alcoholism, since they don't seem to have that term in France.) I kept hoping something would change, but who was I fooling? The short affair petered out anyway because I lived in San Francisco and only got to France occasionally. Once I bought my apartment in Paris, a few years later, I sometimes hoped I'd run into him because we lived in the same neighborhood, but it never happened. And by then I had to ask myself, why did I even entertain the idea of giving it another go?

Last on my list of middle-aged romances was the one when I was fifty-five with a devious scoundrel of a day-trader, who was short on a sense of humor as well as any other saving grace. Why did it take me so long to see this? I guess it was because I couldn't bear to acknowledge that he represented such an awful lapse of judgment on my part. He also had as his daughter, the divine Madeline, to whom I was devoted.

Eventually, if Robert Fisher and I got closer, I knew I'd have to tell him about these misadventures as well as the rest of my checkered past. But what if my story turned him off? I already had more than an inkling that he could be good for me and I didn't want to drive him away.

Since we were just getting to know each other, I would have to think carefully about what to leave in and what to leave out. Would I be in danger of revealing too much on the principle of letting him know the worst right off the bat? Had I already gone overboard in proving I didn't need him because I was fine on my own? Should I tell him about the drugs that ultimately brought me down and the steps that led to my recovery? I was proud that I'd been clean and sober now for 23 years; maybe my history with alcohol would be easier for him to accept than my addiction to cocaine.

I doubted Robert Fisher had had much exposure to the underbelly of the counterculture during the 70s and early 80s. He was a Midwestern suburban man who'd been with one woman. He might not understand how rampant drug-taking had been in my circles. Or that for me drugs had never been a passing fancy or mere experimentation. I'd been born with the addiction gene passed down from both parents and both grandfathers.

When I'd started drinking alcohol at 15, I had a huge beehive hairdo and an older boyfriend. Somehow the ratted mass of sprayed hair made me look older, so I was able to get served at some of the restaurants he took me to. I started out with whisky sours. A sip became a gulp. Alcohol made me feel beautiful and smart. Drinking was fun throughout high school and college, but by the Summer of Love and my days in the Haight Ashbury, it was not considered cool. I hung then mostly with the carefree and adventurous friends I'd grown up with, and with their new friends. We were all experimenting, intent on shedding the staid private school values of our childhoods. It was a rowdy and delightful time. I would definitely tell Robert Fisher all about it, I decided, once he knew me well enough to put it all in perspective.

When I first got divorced, I still thought of drinking as fun, though I began to be aware of some negative aspects. I'd forget what I'd said the night before, forget where I'd parked my car. Then slowly, drinking and drug use started to create lots of problems for me, I didn't always tell the truth, and I couldn't be depended upon by my friends.

But for now, I'd just tell him that I fooled around way too long with drugs after my divorce—just like many people my age in North Beach and elsewhere. Except that I'd taken the involvement further than most—that would be harder to explain. No addict ever intends to become an addict, I wanted him to understand, and that I'd forgiven myself and made my amends. I strongly believed that I wasn't a bad person, but I'd definitely had a bad disease.

My volatile mother had had the addiction disease, too, but she didn't use illegal substances. She took pills prescribed by a doctor, never realizing that her excessive use of drugstore narcotics was a problem. She never found an approach to deal with stress or sorrow other than alcohol or pills. I'd watched her solve her problems that way. I learned that coping device from her early on, even though I vowed never to be like her.

I knew I was lucky to have lived during a time when it became easier for people to admit they needed help. I was forty when I found my way to recovery, and that there was something bigger than I, ultimately in charge.

I definitely wasn't ready to speak to Robert about my last day drinking. It was September 28, 1985. I'd been invited to go to a party with an old friend who'd been after me. I'd go, but I always promised myself if I ever slept with Sam Salgado, that would be my last day drinking. The morning after the party I woke up facing a yellow wall. I tried to raise my pounding head off the pillow to see where the hell I was. It wasn't easy, because my cheek was stuck to the pillowcase. I'd been altogether over-served alcohol

the night before, and I must have snorted my body weight (to borrow a phrase from Annie Lamott) of cocaine. You'll have to use your imagination about the snotty mess that had dried and attached my face to the pillow. Once I'd pulled myself free, I rolled over, and sure enough, there was good old Sam just grinning at me. That was it; that was my last day, and the day my recovery began.

Fortunately, my health hadn't been badly compromised, but I did have a lot of psychological work to do. It's said in certain circles that people don't mature emotionally when they solve problems with substances. That was certainly true for me. For years I'd kept my addictions a secret and it killed me that I couldn't tell the truth about my state of mind. To some people, it was all too obvious. If I hadn't been so consumed with having fun during my thirties, think of all the books I might have read, the music I could have listened to, all the deeper friendships I could have developed. I wished I'd done cooking *étages* in France and Italy, I wished I'd been a better employer and partner. I would have been better off if it hadn't taken me so long to learn how to live well, one day at a time.

I checked the clock; it was 2:00 am. I couldn't turn off

my brain. I wondered what Robert was doing at the same moment. I couldn't wait to start up again with him.

I was thinking about how to describe my parents to Robert Fisher—my dashing, distant father, Paine Knickerbocker, descended from the early settlers of New York, who was, from 1955 to 1974, theater and film critic for *The San Francisco Chronicle* and my beautiful, flirtatious, well-read, political activist mother, Nancy. They were a handsome couple, the Knickerbockers, popular and smart. On weekends they had two cocktail hours, with naps in between. On weekdays, my mother would feel it necessary to have a glass of sherry at 11:30 am in order to summon up the courage to open new bills that arrived in the mail.

Outside her home, my mother treaded two worlds — one in which she worked for fair housing in Black neighborhoods and the other in which she went to cocktail parties and theater openings all done up in taffeta dresses, a gardenia behind her ear. In both these worlds, she flourished, but motherhood was difficult for her. She found me challenging, hard to handle. "Well, what does Madame Fullcharge have to say for herself today?" she'd ask coldly when I came home five minutes late with my starched middy rumpled. But even if I came home early from school, I never knew what mood I'd find her in.

If she'd been out to lunch and had lubricated herself with martinis, she'd be unreasonably demanding or overly demonstrative. On other days, after chairing meetings at the World Affairs Council or the Council for Civic Unity, she'd be the mother I loved and admired. When she felt good about herself, she'd ask me to help her in the kitchen. She trusted me to make vinaigrettes for green salads she served after the main course. Sometimes I made her specialty, Marsala gelée which we called Wine Jell-o. The next day I'd see my mother's little spoon marks in the leftover dessert—it had provided her a way to take a nip without calling it a nip between her weekday sherry and before the cocktail hour.

Did I know my parents were playing with fire when they had a few drinks—when they flirted with people other than each other? Of course, I did, and it devastated me. The kind of behavior they exposed me to seemed wrong and secret, so I never discussed it with anyone except my brother, Tony. Oh. I saw it all. I knew exactly what was going on, I was on guard from the age of eight.

On days when I was sick (or pretending to be sick) and

home from school, I'd answer the phone and find myself talking to mysterious male callers. The voice I heard most often belonged to the suave socialite doctor next door, who had an unmistakable Venezuelan accent. "Is the coast clear?" he'd ask, thinking I was my mother. At dinner one night when I brought this up, my father joked that the doctor had been trying for years to *espalier* my mother against the banister. I couldn't understand why he was trying to make light of it.

Once when my mother was at a fat farm in Mexico, my father came home from a party with a chic blond model. They stumbled up our long flight of stairs, laughing and carrying on, which awakened Tony and me. My father hastily told us to return to bed, but we knew what was going on. It wasn't until after he and my mother had both died, that I heard from a favorite family friend, Sally Lilienthal, that my father had been consistently unfaithful and that my mother's dalliances had largely been in response to his. Probably they'd loved each other and alcohol could, no doubt, be blamed for some of their behavior. But I never heard them talking things over and trying to deal with their problems. Their marriage ran on denial.

There were other marriages like theirs in their

sophisticated social circle. I was only eight when I figured out that the mother of one of my little friends had committed suicide. I was horrified that she'd left her daughter, Sara, my first friend, behind. After that, I kept my eyes peeled because I was worried my mother might try, too. I sensed a certain melancholy and recklessness in her. She actually did try to kill herself when I was fifteen. She'd contracted Hepatitis B on a trip to Spain and couldn't cope with not being able to drink during her recovery. It was all smoothed over and not discussed and, to tell the truth, I didn't feel a great deal of sympathy. I'd seen her drunk and in compromising situations often enough to harden me. Otherwise, I wouldn't have been able to survive.

My awareness of my parents' flirtations—especially my mother's—may have been the reason that when I was twelve, I felt attracted to the first dodgy males I encountered—the Catholic boys from Log Cabin Reform School, who wore pressed blue work shirts and lurked in the last two pews of a church we'd go to when we visited our friends, the Seligmans at a retreat in the Santa Cruz Mountains called the Tree Houses. I loved the thrill of turning my head to look at them and of feeling their gaze upon me. And what about my secret attraction to the rough boys who whistled at me on the street on my walk home from school and were unlike the private school boys I went to dancing class with? Or my willingness to lose my virginity when I was just fifteen on the Naugahyde upholstery of a boyfriend's hot rod car. And why didn't I think that I'd lost anything? The truth was, I'd liked having sex.

I married Jay Hanan at twenty-three in the midst of the Vietnam War, he was a naval officer deployed on an ammunition ship. I was home joining peace marches, substitute teaching, going to rock concerts, and getting stoned. I'd known Jay since high school and loved him for his warmth and his great sense of humor, but after only a couple of years, our relationship was on the rocks. I didn't have a clue about what was driving him and me apart, but I now know a lot of it had to do with my restlessness, our political differences plus the long periods of separation when Jay was at sea. Like my parents, we never tried to work things out or communicate our feelings about the trouble we were in. Among the important issues we never discussed was the crucial question of whether or not we wanted to have kids.

In the summer of 1972, I made Jay breakfast one morning shortly after he returned from a tour of duty.

"This is the last plate of food I'll ever make for you," I told him. He was flabbergasted and I was too. Instead of staying to talk things over, I rolled some joints, headed out the door, and jumped on a waiting yellow motorcycle driven by a bartender friend from Mooney's Irish Pub, where I had just started running my first restaurant with my close pal Flicka McGurrin. She and I'd been the best of friends since we were seven, and we had spent years doing everything together.

CHAPTER FIVE

I'D FINALLY MANAGED TO FALL ASLEEP, but at 3:30 AM, I was wide-awake again. I grabbed my computer, which had been charging on the bed next to me, and propped myself up on my pillows. The kitties stirred and their motors started to rumble. Ready for another round of emails. I wrote:

Good Morning, Robert,

It's 3:30 A.M., and I can't sleep. Why don't you let me know when you are up.

XO, Peggy

I know this is hard to believe, but as I hit the send button, in came a "bing"...You've got mail.

Peggy, I don't know what's going on. I have just been lying here. Please write when you wake up. I am wondering about our dinner plans, should we go on the 13th or 14th, or both? I guess I'll get some coffee and take care of the dogs.

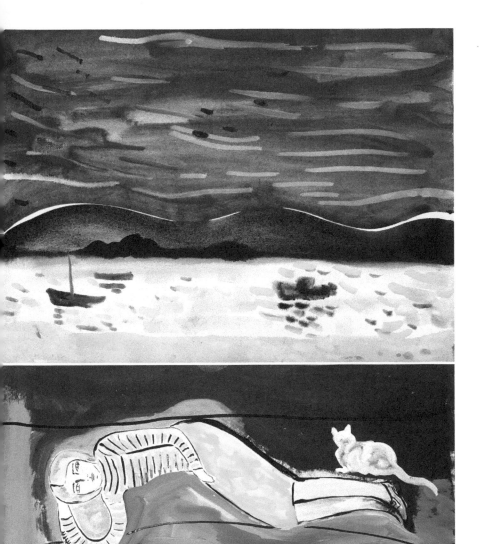

As soon as he returned to his computer, we made a plan to have dinner on the 13th, a couple of weeks away. The 14th was Valentine's Day and he wanted to know if we could get together then as well, but yikes, I didn't want to commit if we didn't get along the first night. I realized that since he hadn't ever dated, that possibility couldn't have occurred to him. And so, I explained that there could be deal-breakers.

"Like what?" he asked.

I pointed out that our chemistry might not work, *"You might wear gold chains or have bad table manners, or worse yet, you might like Céline Dion?"*

He assured me he didn't wear any jewelry and his mother had taught him very good manners. *But what's the matter with Céline Dion?*

I was amazed he took me so seriously. *"Well, if you must know, the problem is that she sings at all. That horrible crinkling of her little nose, her saccharine notes and the way she confuses virtuosity for feelings".*

He shot back, *"Do you have a louder message to follow, or is that it on poor Céline?"*

I wanted to ask him so many questions. But I started with a gentle one. *"I am dying to know more about your children, and how you've spent your days since Bonnie died."*

"I'll tell you first about my recent days. I haven't been alone for 66 years. I loved taking care of Bonnie, she was an extraordinary woman, and now I'm completely lost".

Retreating to safer ground, he told me about his morning routine. He woke early as if he were still going to his office. He drank a lot of cappuccinos. He let the dogs out, all four of them. Then went on to say he read the *New York Times*, the *LA Times*, and *the Journal*—all the way through—and that he loved keeping up with the news. Then his emotions broke through again. *"I haven't really been able to cope. I tried to write thank-you notes for all the condolence letters, but I've just bawled."*

"My friends invite me to dinner, and I talk to my kids constantly. Writing to you is the first spark of life I've felt in three months."

I wanted to bawl, too. He was a seriously sad man. I felt like such a dope for criticizing his taste in music. Without knowing it, he'd paved the way to a deeper conversation by exposing so much about his grief. I could feel my heart opening to him.

Our emails took on a different momentum after that. We began dashing out notes to each other so quickly that spell check didn't have a chance to catch up.

I wanted to know what meals he'd liked as a boy. I asked him about Bonnie's cooking, since I'd learned early on, as soon as I became a food writer, everyone opens up when asked about food.

With that, he asked if he could call me. It was too hard to keep writing. We agreed that we felt more comfortable now. And when the phone rang, I heard his voice as if for the first time. It was like an adolescent's in the way it cracked slightly when the pitch rose. But it had a warm undertone, a persuasive reliability.

"Your voice sounds well-traveled," he told me, "as if you've smoked Camels half your life and drank a lot of whiskey. I had to look at your photograph to be sure you are only 63. You sound like Lauren Bacall on a good day and excuse me for saying it, but a little like a foghorn."

Whiskey, did he say whiskey? The mere mention of it suddenly opened the door for me to go into all the subject matter that had been keeping me awake all night—my drinking and drug use, and my many years of sobriety. Telling Robert wasn't as hard as I'd thought it would be. He said he was sad for me, and then offhandedly told me he hadn't had a drink for years. He told me that drinking wine, as he did, led him to making a series of unwise decisions.

I couldn't believe he didn't drink. I had many friends who did, and I didn't mind, but knew how much easier it would be that we both did not.

We began covering so much ground that we were accidentally interrupting one another. Any remaining ice was broken. We began to reveal vulnerable sides.

Robert's memories of his early years were happy ones. His mother Edna Mae Williams, a Welsh Lutheran turned Catholic, came from a south St. Louis neighborhood where the inhabitants were called 'Scrubby Dutch'— because the women got up early to scrub their front stoops.

She was a hardworking housewife who, along with her mother and aunts, loved to cook big Sunday meals. Robert told me how everyone in the family, including his father Milton, would pitch in to help her. Sometimes they would set up long tables seating twenty to thirty people in his grandparent's basement; pork roasts and dumplings would be served or wild turkeys, rabbits, pheasants, and ducks that his father had shot on hunting expeditions.

Oh boy, did I love that picture. Robert was a born raconteur and what he described to me was what I thought of as real America, real middle America. His stories were just the kind I'd often written for *Saveur.* I told him I couldn't wait to tell Christopher, my friend from the magazine, about his early St. Louis food memories.

In the summer, the men of his mother's side of the family would dig a huge open pit in the yard. They'd drink beer together as they cooked ribs, chicken, and sausages. Robert went into detail about his favorite German potato salad and the cabbage and greens that would go with the grilled meats.

It had barely started to get light outside, on the second day of our communication, and he was going on about the way baseball games had blared from a crackly old radio perched on the porch on hot St. Louis afternoons. I loved his description of the relatives who adored him when he was little: "The women, in cotton aprons and white socks covering their sturdy ankles, switched from apple pies in the winter to cherry pies during the summer, topped with Velvet Freeze vanilla ice cream from the corner store."

All this was music to my ears. I wished I had been part of such a family. When I asked about his father, he told me, "He was a charmer, a dreamer. He was a self-made man, Jewish, and a serial entrepreneur. He ended up with a great collection of post-war contemporary art." Robert choked as he remembered his father, whom he called *"My all-time*

best friend." He'd always looked up to him, even when his dad left his mother. Robert was only 14 at the time, and his brother Richard was away in college.

I told him that our families couldn't have been less alike, explaining that mine had consisted of only the four of us, with no extended family except a couple of aunts who lived in New York and Chicago. And although my mother's cooking was very good, it was tame in comparison to his mother's. Nancy Knickerbocker's specialties had been roasted legs of lamb with mint sauce, lemon caper veal, and the occasional *boeuf bourguignon*. She gave everything a French name and considered herself a gourmet cook. She loved to read Gourmet Magazine at lunchtime. We always had dinner in our red dining room with candles on the table and in the reflection lots of polished silver. No fire pits in our garden. And we never had desserts.

"*No desserts? Why not? You make desserts, don't you?*" Robert said in an alarmed voice. I assured him that I made very good ones, mostly when friends came over. I explained that both my parents had always watched their waistlines. "I hope you don't watch yours," he said.

My God, no man had ever said anything like that to me! I'd felt fat, ever since I was fifteen, when my father told me I was putting on too much weight. ("You are fat, Peggy.") Maybe he'd needed new glasses. I was five-feet seven inches tall and only weighed 115-120 pounds, but he had my mother take me to a doctor for diet pills the next day. Before that, he'd always called me "lovely."

I had a perfect figure as a young girl and never really had a weight- problem, but I didn't feel perfect until Robert said, "Hope you don't watch yours." That was a milestone for me. Could I finally stop holding in my stomach?

"We're going to have to have a long conversation about desserts," Robert was saying, "but I'd rather tell you more about my childhood, Peggy, since it seems so different from yours. You see, I always felt adored by both parents, even after they divorced. I never doubted myself as a kid."

"Lucky you," I said. "I felt loved, but I wouldn't say adored." I was mostly proud of my parents, but they were usually too busy being intellectual and captivating, to help me feel confident and secure. We had our best times together as a family on summer vacations. I told Robert that it was my father to whom I'd felt particularly close. When I was a little girl, I'd sit in the bay window of our living room waiting for him to turn the corner on his way home from work. He'd be in a jacket with a bachelor button in his lapel and always wore a tie and a hat. I'd race down our long staircase with my dachshund flying after me and dash out the door to greet him.

I felt a little jealous when Robert told me how his mother used to awaken him every morning. "She'd come into my room with a hot washcloth for my face." His freshly ironed school clothes would be hanging from her arm and as he dressed, she'd run out to the bakery and bring home a hot gooey peanut coffee cake.

My brother Tony and I had been on our own in the mornings. Not that we starved. We got ourselves up when our clock radios turned on with the songs of Little Richard or Elvis. I often ironed my school uniform, a white middy that I wore over a blue skirt. I'd been the one who made toast for Tony and me, or poured us bowls of Sugar Frosted Flakes. I'd always felt this was normal until I heard Robert's story.

Before I left for school, I told Robert, it was my job to bring my mother's breakfast on a tray along with the society page from the San Francisco Chronicle. She'd be sitting up in bed in her pale blue velvet bed jacket with Certainly Red lipstick slashed across her thin lips. She kept the lipstick in her bedside drawer along with Mentholatum ointment,

Lubriderm hand cream, and a jar of Phenobarbital. Accompanying her cup of strong Lipton's tea would be a piece of white toast, exactly the way she liked it, with cinnamon sugar sprinkled over cold butter.

"Each day I'd make lunch for myself—sandwiches with the crusts cut off so I could be like the other girls in my class who had cooks at home preparing their lunches."

Robert said, "You were doing that as my mother was making me egg bun sandwiches with braunschweiger and bologna and Tabasco. But that's such a tender detail about the bread crusts, Peggy."

By this time, we were thoroughly warmed up. I realized that only two people who were falling for each other would have cared about the kinds of sandwiches each of us had brought to school.

CHAPTER SIX

I GOT BACK TO MY ROUTINE the next day, meeting my exercise pals to climb the Lyon Street Steps. Up and down on a crisp clear February morning—the Japanese plum trees in blossom, the bay still and steely. High on endorphins, I had a grin on my face and a lilt to my step. Was I falling in love? Of course not. My God! Not so soon! That would have been insane, and I knew it. My friends knew it too, but they were all ears and wanted details.

By the time I got home, I had a few calls to return. During the last few days, I'd spent so much time talking to Robert that my messages had piled up. When I'm not available, my friends start to wonder.

Christopher was happy for me when I explained what had been going on. She listened to my excited account of the family meals Robert ate in his youth. I could tell she wanted to interrupt and say, "Yes, but you haven't met him, Peggy." But she restrained herself, and that was one more reason to love her so much. Nobody wanted me to get hurt. I knew I should go low and slow, as I say when I cook a pork roast. But this time, there had been no red flags, no obfuscations. His determined pursuit made me feel steady, reassured.

It doesn't take most women sixty-three years to learn that if a relationship doesn't feel right at first, it probably won't later. This one felt right. I'd always thought I could change the course of a love affair, or worse, change the man. With Robert Fisher, that was not the case. Nothing he'd said to me so far made me think I even needed to tinker.

I called Flicka and Cammie Conlon, my beloved sponsor, to let them know how things were going. To tell the truth, I told anyone who'd listen to my first impressions of Robert. "Keep me posted," a few of my friends responded. "Careful Peggy," is what they meant. My brother, Tony said, "I'm happy for you but please don't make your family suffer through another disaster." Their cautious reactions didn't match mine at all. They didn't understand, this guy was different.

I would soon learn that Robert's children, his therapists—one in LA and another in St. Louis—and his friends thought he'd gone over the deep end. They were not amused. Neither was his 95-year-old mother-in-law in Florida who had been mourning for only three months. Never mind that Bonnie had been very sick for almost five years. Nobody wanted to hear his absurd claims about falling in love so quickly. His children were furious with him.

Back on the phone with me, Robert sounded as though he fully assumed we were going to be together. While I might have taken his certainty as a compliment, I knew he had come to it recklessly. We'd only had a few days of communication. There was still the big question of how we'd feel when we finally laid eyes on one another. Even so, I couldn't help feeling high. We laughed when we heard each other's voices.

Then Robert said, "If this feels so different for you, so different from ALL the others, I wonder if you would have been attracted to me when you were younger, say fifteen years ago."

I had to admit that I still wasn't sure I was going to be attracted to him now. For the twentieth time, I repeated,

"We haven't met, Robert."

But he blew off the thought. "In case you hold any lingering doubts about me being a dog, I've Fed Exed a photograph to you."

When the package came, I ripped it open and took a long look at him. Now that I could put a face to his voice, he was not what I'd pictured at all. Not that I could remember exactly what I'd pictured. No, he wasn't a dog. But he looked so serious. He was a good-looking man, in a stern, academic way. His gaze was earnest, not as warm as I'd have expected. His hair was short, receding. That was fine. I liked bald. But the photograph disquieted me. He didn't look like my eager, romantic, slightly wild guy on the other end of the phone.

No, he wasn't the Robert Fisher I'd imagined. On the tip of his nose, small round tortoise-shell glasses perched— almost as a prop, I thought.

"They are not props at all," Robert said sounding a bit irritated at the thought. "They are real glasses and I have them in every color."

I asked why, when he went to the trouble of posing for a professional photograph, he hadn't tried to look a little warmer, a little more smiley.

He told me the reason for the stern look on his face. The photo had been taken on a day when he and Bonnie had one of their rare arguments as they drove up Highway One to Big Sur to visit their old St. Louis friend, the photographer Bob Kolbrenner. They were both still feeling glum when they posed for their individual portraits.

I kept staring at Robert's portrait as he talked and found myself warming up to his likeness. Now I could see him as I heard him speak.

A day or so before he was to come to San Francisco, he called me while driving one of his dogs to the vet. He was on the 405 Freeway when he suddenly dropped his phone. I could hear barking. I went a little crazy over the fact that that he didn't have a listening device, that he was driving while talking, trying to control his dog and he probably had a coffee in his hand, too.

He regained his composure and got ready to drop a bomb. "I have a very serious question for you." And without drawing breath, he said, "I want to marry you. I'd like to ask you to marry me. Will you?"

I was speechless. He told me he was totally in love. He had found his match. He was positive. "Will you?" he asked again after only a few days of conversation.

Gasping for air, I reacted strongly, "Robert, are you kidding? Have you gone out of your mind?" I didn't wait for an answer, "Apparently so," I continued. "You are a delight, you're enchanting. But you are scaring me! Have you gone off your meds?"

He wanted to know the last time that someone had proposed. I told him that the proposal was completely out of bounds. We could not discuss anything about the future until we met.

Shit, I thought. Another huge mistake. I've done it again. I have landed another impossible man. This time it's a man who likes me too much. He's rash, totally unreasonable.

I felt shaken, almost sick. How could I not have recognized he was such a screwball?

"May we agree to discuss this when you arrive," I said stiffly, "and not bring it up again until a sensible amount of time has passed?"

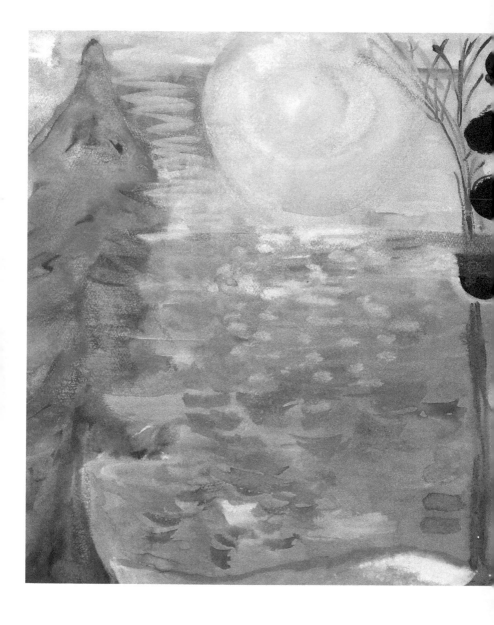

CHAPTER SEVEN

ROBERT LET THE MARRIAGE DISCUSSION GO and didn't bring it up again. We were two days away from meeting. I had to remain occupied, so I busied myself around the house. The weather was gray and gloomy, and I needed flowers, lots of them. I was in luck. Spring comes early in Northern California, and masses of pale blossoms filled the farmers' market flower stalls. Even though I'm a native, I'm always caught off guard by the precocious appearance of tulips, daffodils, and fragrant fruit-tree blooms. I bought armloads.

Hot pink quince blossoms went into an orange-and-gold vase on my lamb-sized butcher block in the entryway. There they would greet Robert Fisher—a man I had yet to meet. Tulips and daffodils went in the living room, bunches of paperwhite narcissus and sprigs of Daphne went beside my bed and on the bathroom sink. Had I overdone it just a tiny bit? Did the splashy arrays verge on funereal?

A sinker hit me, out of the gray chill of the day, the unmistakable dread that it was going to be the same old story, that whatever we'd started wouldn't work out. The whole idea had been such a stretch, to begin with. Although now I honestly thought romance was probably not in the cards, I proceeded as if it were. Since my concentration was shot, I decided to distract myself instead of trying to write, I walked a few blocks over to Chestnut Street and bought a nice new pair of jeans that fit well except for being tight around the waist.

Robert called early the morning of February 11th with an update. His friends Paige and Michael Doumani knew about the hundreds of emails, texts, and phone calls between us and were concerned that the romance was altogether too much, too soon. No shit. They insisted he go out on one date with another woman before meeting me, so he'd be coming a day later than originally planned.

"Well, maybe they are right," I said after Robert had explained. "And doesn't one of your daughters have someone she wants you to meet in the future? Take all the time you want," I said in my least convincing voice.

"Do I hear a note of irony?" Robert asked.

After I admitted I did feel a little jealous about his blind date the following evening, he immediately said that right after he'd taken her to dinner, he would drive up to San Francisco.

My jealousy instantly melted. "What a gallant gesture," I remember saying.

The night of his arrival, I had dinner—if you could call it that, because I was incapable of swallowing—with three close women friends. I was in a swoon, walking on air, way, way above earth. Robert's visit dominated the conversation. We all shrieked and laughed, considering various dénouements. I wore, for their approval, what I would greet him in: my new jeans and a crisp white shirt. I worried about how the jeans fit around my waist. I couldn't really breathe, but everyone said they looked great.

Barbara Mendelsohn, who knew how to fix anything, took one look at me and said, "Take your pants off."

I surrendered them. Barbara put her gleaming black

leather boot on the waistband and started to pull and stretch it with her heel. She told me she was making the waist looser, to make my soufflé top disappear. "Robert will be able to put his arm around you and not feel a bulge."

I put the pants back on and asked her to hug me around my waist like someone who was glad to see me. Her trick worked.

All of them gave me tips. They told me that if I didn't like Robert, I didn't need to invite him for the night; I had waited so long to meet someone, that if this wasn't right, I could just wait longer, carry on as I was. I knew I'd probably ignore this advice. But I felt reassured by their warmth and their humor. No matter what happened, I would always have my precious friends.

I returned home, full of anticipation. My house awaited Robert Fisher. The wood in the living room fireplace, just off my little garden, was ready to light. I'd filled a pale green bowl with Satsuma tangerines and put it on the café table in my kitchen. My favorite cheeses, a present from my friends at Cowgirl Creamery, were softening on the kitchen counter. The coffee beans were fresh and ready to be ground. One morning I'd heard Robert on his cell ordering a triple cappuccino at Starbucks. My kind of guy.

I knew he'd be very late—even without traffic, San Francisco is a good 5-1/2 to 6 hours' drive from LA. And so, a little later that evening, I slid between freshly pressed sheets to rest. But all I did was thrash around.

I must have dozed off because when the phone rang, I was groggy as I reached for it. We'd agreed, Robert would call once he saw the windmills at the Altamont Pass, about an hour away.

It was nearly 2:30 a.m. "I brought lots of chocolate to keep me awake, but I'm so excited, I haven't eaten a bite," he said on the phone. I was excited, too, but I still had all my doubts. He had none.

I asked about his date.

"Well, I suppose she was very nice and pretty, but I was only thinking about you."

"Yes, but what was she like?" I asked as I turned on the water for my bath.

"She wore very large clip-on earrings and looked over my shoulder the whole time at other people in the restaurant. Besides, she just came in from a golf game, and she's probably a Republican."

"Is that all?" I asked.

"No," he said. "She's been dating on Match.com and

told me she often left her car running outside a café as she dashed in to check out a prospective date."

A few minutes later, I threw on the clothes that I'd left on a chair near my bed. I was sweating, because the bath had been so hot, and

because I was excited. Downstairs, I lit the fire and turned down the lights to the dimmest setting. I unwrapped the cheeses and ground the coffee. And then sooner than I'd expected, I heard him knocking on the door. I walked toward it hesitantly, thinking of all the single women who'd know what I was going through at that moment.

I took a deep breath then let it all go. I opened the door. There he was, a large, willing bald man, smiling at me. We just looked at each other. I bowed my head. I felt shy. Sweat dripped down my waist and off my brow. He had so many packages in his arms that he was a little hard to make out. He came in, dropped them on the sofa, and gave me a huge hug.

We both shuddered, in the best imaginable way. We went into the kitchen, I made him a cappuccino, a triple. He was warm, easy to talk to, and looked good in his navy-blue sweater. Before we went any further, I told him that there'd been a rash of car break-ins on my street and suggested that he bring in his suitcase. So, he went out to his car to get his luggage—six large black matching bags. It took him a couple of trips. "I guess you like to be prepared," I joked, "Just stash them in the dining room."

We returned to the kitchen where I could get a good look at him. His head was shaved and his glasses were round. He smelled great and his face was soft. He was a big guy; muscular, mid-western-grass-fed, and, as I far as could make out in the dim light, his eyes were blue-gray. He was all man and did I love that?

"You look great but quite different from the headshot you sent," he said, smiling. "I'm not at all disappointed, but when was that picture taken?"

"Maybe five years ago," I admitted. "Well, gosh, wait a minute, maybe fourteen years—but then again it could have been taken twenty years ago." I felt embarrassed, but he was lighthearted about it.

By the way he looked at me now, I knew that none of this mattered. "You are it," he said, "I just knew you would be."

My whole body went into a blush. He was not afraid to let me know how he felt, in person. I could not think of any reason to hold back.

And so, after our two-week epistolary romance—a torrent of words in which we'd discussed everything from politics (it was right before the 2008 primaries: he was for Obama and I was still for Hillary) to our love of Paris, our families, our favorite artists and writers, our animals, eating habits, and restaurants, and the fact that neither of us drank—here we were in the middle of the night, knowing what we knew. I was right in thinking it was all out of my control. My thoughts were swirling, and rather than let them interfere with our time, I just let go, again. He was so utterly aflame, I could have melted into a puddle on the floor.

We sat at the kitchen table finishing our coffees. He told me he was charmed by my old Italian coffee pot and the way I frothed milk on the top of the stove. Then he went into the living room to get the presents he'd brought me. An orange Hermes scarf (he'd asked me my favorite color), a speaker for my iPod, and my first iPhone. Yikes. It was like my birthday. His grin indicated he was getting a boyish pleasure out of my delight. I couldn't help but remember my only present from the last man in my life: a couple of pairs of pathetic little socks for Christmas, from the bottom of a sales bin. I felt a tiny bit awkward and overwhelmed. And undeserving, too, given how briefly we'd known each other. But I loved his generosity and wasn't exactly shy about tearing open his presents, letting the wrapping paper fall to the floor. He'd brought along family albums, as well.

Then I suggested we go sit in the living room, where it was more comfortable. We settled into the cushiony sofa in front of the fire. And pretty soon we were making out. I don't know about him, but I felt like a sixteen-year-old. It was a relief, it was awkward, and it was passionate.

A little later on, Robert showed me photographs of his family—his children and grandchildren and Bonnie. There were pictures of his dogs, too. He became emotional and pretty raw as we looked at all of them. Most of the shots were old and small. I had the urge to get a magnifying glass to get a better look at Bonnie, but this wasn't the time to do that. She looked natural and lovely. His voice caught a few times when he talked about her long battle with brain and kidney cancer, and his vulnerability made him all the more appealing.

He explained that she'd gone into brain surgery and came out a completely altered person who would endure months of being comatose, bedridden, unable to speak or see clearly. Finally, she was totally paralyzed. All of this occurred, he told me, after two operations on her brain, gallbladder, shin, both adrenal glands, and she endured the insertion of shunts and filters to avoid blood clots. "I slept in her room at the hospital many nights," he said.

He needed to talk, to get this all out. I was speechless as he described starting to grieve in the examination room the day after her first operation when the doctor told her, "You are going to die."

Robert went on to say that he failed to understand what was happening to him but that he felt "emotionally ravaged and stripped of anything I knew the day before."

He was of the opinion that grieving is one of the least understood, and at the same time, predictable human emotions. And our emotions, Robert's and mine, were flying in every direction. We both felt so much after the first few weeks of correspondence. There was no putting a hold on what was happening.

We held each other for what seemed like five minutes. The energy between us was about to ignite. I kept stalling because I was hesitant and the moment was so heavy and sad. And then we looked at each other as if to say, 'This is the moment'. What the hell, I thought, it's not as if I'll get pregnant and I knew him a lot better than some men I'd slept with.

We climbed the stairs. The kitties trailed us, then bounded up before us. I kept reminding myself he'd never been with any woman but his wife. From my bedroom window, the searchlights of Alcatraz streamed across the water, and fishing boats followed the path they lit out of the bay to the Pacific Ocean. The view was pretty stunning, but I must admit it was not foremost in either of our thoughts.

I'm not sure what I expected, but when Robert got on his knees in my bedroom, I became a little alarmed. But it turned out he was looking for a plug for my new speaker. I guessed he wanted to set the mood. He inserted his iPod and scrolled the menu patiently until he reached Diana Krall. I couldn't believe how slow and measured he was. He carefully took off his clothes, folding them neatly— shirt, boxers, and knee-high socks. His polished shoes went, side by side, under the chair. I felt more inclined to rip my clothes off, just like the wrapping paper. And I flung them about the room, feeling a little silly in my show of passionate abandon.

We faced each other as bare-ass naked as we were on

our first days on earth. Bulges could not have mattered less. We didn't notice anything but skin. The words of the song, "Let's Fall in Love," urged us on. In bed, we were hardly bashful, but time did not stand still, nor did the earth shake. Neither of us cared. We were in our sixties.

The next half hour could best be described as purposeful and fervent. Then we fell dead asleep, holding one another. I knew it was 6:00 a.m. because the cable car clanged by and the newspapers hit the front porch with a thud. The kitties sniffed around and started purring, wanting my attention, but they seemed to like my overnight guest as much as I did. I kept my eyes shut, waiting for what was next.

More of the same! Not bad for a sixty-six-year-old guy who was a bit out of shape.

Day broke. It was sunny. From my bedroom window, the bay looked flat and still as it does during the winter. "It's the best time for rowing boats," I told him. "Maybe we could take a walk, a little later, to the Dolphin Club? It's my old-fashioned swimming and rowing club down at the water. I'd love to show it to you." Now he noticed the view for the first time and was delighted with it.

Downstairs and dressed, we drank more hot steamy

coffee and devoured warm buttered blueberry muffins. We'd worked up an appetite. I cooked some asparagus, fried a couple of eggs in olive oil, and put them on top of toast with some grated Parmesan. Everything ran together lusciously when we broke the yolks. The transition between being courted and being made love to had been seamless.

He thanked me for listening to his story about Bonnie. We'd been together for a mere four hours, but you could have fooled me.

It was time to get some fresh air. And so, we bundled up and walked down the street to the beach, grabbing for each other's hands. I felt so good, I stopped along the way to tell a house painter he was doing a great job. That seemed to please Robert. We were in a state of grace. Luckily, we wore sunglasses, because everything glinted— the fisherman's line casting off the pier and the splatter of surf lapping the beach.

I took him into my swimming club, a club anyone can join, and where I have been a member for so long that my photograph is up on the wall with the other old-timers. We wandered into the boat room and looked at the old wooden boats, shiny with varnish, then we peeked into the tiny blue-and-white galley, smelling of just-fried bacon and coffee. Robert was astonished when a shivering swimmer came out of the water, which in February was around forty-eight degrees. I explained that I went in the water between March and November and even then, mostly on sunny days. In foggy San Francisco, that didn't leave me much time to swim.

From the old-fashioned weight room next door, donated years ago by Jack LaLanne, we could hear grunts and groans from members working out on the squeaky old machinery. Robert was amazed to hear that LaLanne once swam from Alcatraz, towing a rowboat, attached to a heavy chain, by his teeth.

We walked the three blocks home, smooching along the way. Robert told me my house reminded him of a French country inn. He was such a romantic. He said he'd never thought he'd be this happy again.

When the twelve o'clock whistle blew, it was time for lunch. I took him to another of my haunts, Swan Oyster Depot, where I have been going a couple of times a week since I was a girl.

Robert drove us there. The cheery owners, the Sanchimino brothers, who also swam at the Dolphin Club, greeted us. I ordered my usual: a Dungeness crab cocktail with mayonnaise on the side and a couple of heels of bread. It was good, shiny, dark-baked Boudin sourdough that goes so well with crab, and just about anything. Robert ordered my usual, too, and we shared a platter of Kumamoto oysters with horseradish and a dash of red sauce.

See's Candy was next door. My usual routine was to have a nice lunch filled with protein at Swan, and then saunter into See's for a few pieces of chocolate for dessert. Robert loved the suggestion, so we ordered a bag full of dark creamy brown sugar flavored Bordeaux candies, eating them all up by the time we got back to his SUV.

Later that afternoon, Robert had to drive down to Stanford for a memorial service for an old friend. He was going to be in Palo Alto for the next 24 hours. He grabbed a kiss while he took the things he'd need out of his six Prada bags. He'd thrown them in the dining room, out of the way, when he arrived. "Why 6 bags, how long are you staying anyway?" I teased him about them mercilessly, because I thought they were a bit showy. He got them out of my way and snatched his toiletry kit from the one small bathroom in the house, along with his toothbrush that had been in a glass next to mine.

"I didn't know what we'd be doing," Robert said, "and I just kept grabbing things as I loaded my car. You'll get used to me, one of my close friends calls me Maximum Bob." I accepted his answer, but his friend was right, Robert was a little over the top. Besides, he had his life to return to in LA, so I knew he had no intention of staying with me long.

Then it was time for him to go. He looked dashing in a navy-blue suit with a crisp white shirt and polished shoes. Just like my father, my all-time favorite dresser, he wore a paisley silk square in his breast pocket. He'd be back tomorrow, Valentine's Day, to take me to dinner at Zuni.

CHAPTER EIGHT

I WAS LYING ON MY BED READING when I heard Robert at the door—I'd left it unlocked for him. He let himself in and bounded up the stairs. He was wound-up, exuberant, like a kid after a sugary birthday party.

"Get up," he said, "get up, we're going out for dinner! It's Valentine's Day, and I have a present for you." He gave me a big kiss and asked, "Do you want it now or later?"

"Now, of course. What is it?"

He handed me a very large box with a wide silk ribbon tied in a floppy bow.

Oh no, I thought, not a mink coat. He'd be capable of giving me one—the only problem was, I was hardly the type.

But it wasn't a mink coat. It was a good-looking green army jacket made by an Italian designer. I love clothes and giving me this jacket struck a chord. It was damn handsome. I tried it on, and it looked great.

"Wow, I've never had anything quite like this," I told him. "I love it, thank you. I've never been given presents like yours," I told him as we got dressed like an old married couple. "I am so touched. All I've given you is a faxed photograph of my legs, a blueberry muffin, and some asparagus on toast."

I felt excited about walking into Zuni with Robert. I'd so often walked in there alone. Bob Carrau, played the piano there a couple of nights a week, and tonight was one of them. When I'd told him that we were coming in, Bob had suggested I ask Robert for the names of a few of his favorite songs. He'd learn them in advance, he promised, if he didn't know them already. I was delighted to have the two meet. Bob, his partner Tony, and I often cooked for each other and we'd all traveled together. He'd been happy to hear I had a Valentine.

He spotted us through the window as we got out of Robert's car. As soon as we entered the restaurant, we heard Bob playing "It Could Happen to You." Robert was touched when I told him it was for us.

We were shown to the table I'd requested by the window. Bob had said he'd come over during his break.

We ordered San Pellegrino and Zuni's version of a Caesar, the best in town, along with some house-cured anchovies. As we started buttering our Acme bread, Robert asked me where I wanted to go on our first trip.

"Berlin or Vietnam," I said.

"Could we include Singapore?" he asked. He started telling me about it as Bob slid into our banquette. Robert told him, after the introductions, what we had just been talking about. "I'll only take Peggy first class," he blurted out. "Nothing else is good enough for her."

That made me feel uncomfortable. It seemed a little boastful. Bob and I were well aware that when I traveled, except for work, I paid for my own trips, I didn't go First Class unless I had enough accumulated miles, and even then, I'd usually choose Business.

Robert was complimentary about the music Bob played, and about being at Zuni. It was such a great spot—delicious and fun. It had been around for thirty years and still attracted the young and the old, the hip and the stodgy. I'm not exactly sure what the two men talked about because I wasn't listening. I felt wedged between the comfort of what I'd had with Bob and our group of friends, my life as it had been for the past decade, and on the brink of something new. I felt a shock of ambiguity, a *soupçon* of joy and fear.

Meanwhile, Robert was on an ascent talking a mile a minute. I wondered how he'd fit into my life as I knew and loved it.

Returning to the piano, Bob broke into "Let's Fall in Love," another of Robert's requests. Now the two of us were suddenly in real time. Here we were face-to-face, grownups out to dinner on the most romantic night of the year. Robert was darling, touching, almost feverish as he grabbed me and kissed me and looked into my eyes. He was coming on so strong, in fact, I had a hard time with all the intense gazing. If I hadn't known better, I'd have thought he was using coke. But then I always thought an extrovert was using coke, just like some of my gay friends think everyone's gay.

I usually felt shy with new men, or too animated, nodding my head a little too agreeably. I didn't feel shy with Robert, but suddenly I felt a little resistance. Was he going to be this eager all the time?

Then Robert told me solemnly, "What I am really doing on this trip is trying to put some closure to my life with Bonnie. I thought of the idea before I ever heard your name. We came to San Francisco for our honeymoon in 1963, stayed at the Fairmont, and ate at restaurants that are no longer here—The Blue Fox, Amelio's, and Ernie's. Then we went to the Highland Inn in Carmel and on down the coast to Santa Barbara. I am retracing our steps."

"That's lovely in theory, but isn't meeting me and remembering Bonnie at the same time, conflicting for you?" I asked.

He told me he didn't look at it that way. "It's putting closure on what was and exploring what is real today. And I can't move forward with you until I come to grips with my loss." He went on to say that his memories would never leave him.

"I can appreciate that," I said. "I have deep respect for a long happy marriage and all the memories that accompany it. I am delighted to say I find being with you quite thrilling. But you know this all takes a while, don't you?"

"Not for me, it doesn't," Robert insisted. "I knew how I felt even before I met you, and I feel it now more intensely." That response ruffled my feathers, made me feel uneasy. His leap of faith was absurd and one day he'd realize it. It didn't take care of me, it was his fantasy, not mine.

I was surprised to learn that evening that Robert's mother, like mine, had been an alcoholic. Robert told me that it got to the point where he and Bonnie couldn't trust her to babysit their children because they would often find her slurring her words and unsteady on her feet at the end of an evening.

I told Robert how I'd come home from school, never knowing in what condition I'd find my mother. If it was before 5:00 she would usually be fine, but after 5:00, it would be touch and go. I didn't know that my father's drinking was as problematic until the night he invited me to accompany him, to a fancy dinner for the great Norwegian actress Liv Ullman. I was about twenty-five when I noticed. That night, he'd had several drinks plus the wine that was being poured. At one point when I looked over at my dear dad, his head had dropped perilously close to his soup bowl. I shrieked across the table at him just before his head nodded and made a splash.

My father's disease became dramatically clear when he was in his early sixties, the age I am now. He had to have an eye operation and was required to go 24 hours pre-op without a drink. As he was on the gurney rolling into the operating room, he got the DTs. A nurse administered alcohol intravenously to stop his shakes. It was a good thing, Robert and I agreed, that neither of us drank anymore.

By the time Robert and I finished Zuni's divine roasted chicken for two, I could feel myself in danger again of losing the battle to put on the brakes. Was I speaking loudly enough, was I being heard?

As we were winding down by sharing a plate of cookies, Robert told me once more that he knew he loved me and asked me if I thought I would love him any time soon.

"Robert," I said, "this is just our first dinner. Let's have the time of our lives and take it all with a tiny grain of salt."

"Oh bullshit," he said, and asked for the bill.

"I'd like to split it with you," I said, reaching for my bag.

"What are you talking about? I'm taking care of this! That's the way I like to do it."

Uh oh, I thought. I guess he's not exactly the feminist he claims to be.

Once back in the car, he asked if I minded stopping at the Fairmont Hotel. He assumed he'd be spending the night at my house, he said, but he just wanted to walk into the lobby and take a look at the room he'd reserved a few weeks ago—the one where he'd spent part of his honeymoon in 1963. He needed to see what it felt like without Bonnie and asked if I would join him.

The whole idea sounded mad to me, and I didn't want to participate in his closure. I have problems with the word *closure*, which is something therapists always want you to come back for after you've decided to stop seeing them. I don't really believe in it. In Robert's case, I supposed he was dealing with his grief as best he could, and I respected his need to go through that process.

"I'll stay here, but take your time," I said. So, I waited in the car singing along with Diana Krall, "Let's Fall in Love," as the red caution lights blinked.

It was cold and windy on Nob Hill. There was no longer much activity around the Fairmont. The top of the hill wasn't the gay old nightspot it once was in my parent's day and my youth. Young people and business types preferred the action South of Market. I, too, had a long history with the Fairmont. Cal's family had owned the hotel until recently. I'd spent one night of my own honeymoon there with Jay all those years ago and couldn't recall the room number. But there was no need to bring that up with Robert. Tonight, was his deal.

When he returned about twenty minutes later, his eyes were red, and he seemed shaken. "That was quite an experience," he said. "I just stood there in the dark, then sat on the bed looking out the window. I missed having that moment with her. I missed her. I really didn't think I could go on when she died. And now I know I can."

I wanted to cry, too. "Do you really want to spend the night in the room you reserved?" I asked. "I can't imagine what being there did to your heart. These must have been twenty of the strangest minutes either of us has spent."

"I am all over the place, in case you haven't noticed," Robert said. "Let's head back to your house."

And so, we did. We drove the few blocks home to Russian Hill in silence. My street was quiet too, the fog was rolling in, and I knew I was already sinking into this romance more quickly than was comfortable. I badly needed some oxygen. An awful lot had just happened.

We didn't talk much before we fell into bed. We were both exhausted. I put on my new black lace nightie and slid under the covers. That did the trick—we still had enough energy for passion as it turned out.

CHAPTER NINE

W E WOKE AT 6:00 the next morning with the cats meowing, the cable car clanging, newspapers hitting the door. Robert asked what I was going to do that day.

In case he thought I was going to devote my day to him, I felt it best to let him know right off the bat that I had plans. "I'm going to meet some friends at Crissy Field where we'll walk along the water to the Bridge. Then I'll stop for coffee in a little café next door to my meeting. And after that, I'll probably come home and call my nephew Keary for his birthday and get ready to go to a meeting for Slow Food Nation."

"Can I tag along on the walk with you and go with you to your meeting?" Robert asked me as I crawled out of bed.

"Well sure," I said a little reluctantly. "It's usually just women, but I know they're dying to meet you. Make sure to wear warm clothes—you must have some in one of those fancy bags of yours."

I was downstairs making coffee when Robert appeared in the blue and white Dolphin Club-sweatshirt I'd left for him as a tiny Valentine present on top of one of his Prada bags. He wore white sneakers and socks and heavy sweatpants, gathered at the ankles. We drank our coffee at home and drove off with the sun coming up to our east and over the crest of Lombard and Hyde Streets. I'd texted Barbara Mendelsohn, of the shiny black boots that stretched my jeans, to ask her to tell the others he was going to join us for the walk.

During the morning walk with my friends, Robert talked to Barbara about sports, and I could tell she was impressed, since she was a huge baseball and football fan. He was excited to learn that Janet Dalton was a pastry chef and confessed to having a sweet tooth. He fit right in. I was amazed by his utter lack of self-consciousness. He had a well-developed feminine side and was eloquent and charming. I was proud to have them meet him.

After the walk, Robert and I parted with my friends

and went on our way to a little café near my meeting. He bought coffees and sweets and then we went next door to settle in. He identified with people's stories and seemed comfortable enough. Again, I was happy to have him with me, but he was wedging himself into the tightest spaces in my life.

Afterward, we drove home, and I got ready to start my day. While I bathed and dressed, he sat in the living room, in a tiny patch of sun, reading the paper and drinking his fourth or fifth coffee. After straightening up around the house, I found that the patch of sun had moved, but Robert had not. He was still sitting in the orange leather chair by the garden, starting in on the second paper, with Lola purring on his lap. As he finished a section, he'd drop it on the floor. It was as if he'd moved in permanently. I began to wish he'd go. We definitely needed time off from each other.

I went into my office and called my nephew Keary, who lived in Portland, to wish him a Happy Birthday. I was dying to hear the latest about his young daughter Amelia. Then I started gathering my notes and folders for the Slow Food meeting.

Robert hadn't made a sound downstairs, hadn't

budged an inch. I told him I was finished in the bathroom if he'd like to bathe. "Oh no, thank you. I am just fine here, catching up on my emails," he said, his BlackBerry in his hand.

I realized that a man who had never dated didn't know the rules—the adult sleep-over rules: Don't answer the host's phone and make yourself scarce the morning after. Today those rules struck me as wise. I wanted to play by the old North Beach Beat customs when love was freer and so were we. I realized that Robert had no place to go, but I wasn't used to having someone hanging around.

I was getting a little worked up, annoyed. I needed my space. I wanted my house back. I wanted to think about what had happened since he'd arrived. I needed to call my friends for some feedback and reinforcement. I had to weigh what was going on. I also knew I was being unreasonable.

I marched downstairs. He was chuckling away at a message on his phone, happy as a clam. God help me. I wanted this to work out, but I wanted him to say good-bye for now. I lived alone. I was used to having my house to myself.

"Robert, no offense, but I have to start my day," I said

tensely. "What are your plans?"

Is this an old pattern, I wondered? Am I treating him like the other failed relationships? Wham bam, thank you, man. Could I not handle the closeness, did I not know how? Would I feel this way if a woman were staying over? No. He was a man in whom I was interested, but I wanted a bit of mystery. I wanted him to have something to do, somewhere to go, to be more independent.

"Oh, well, I'll get out of your hair. I didn't know I was in the way. I have a lunch scheduled with Steve Grand-Jean and Bob Jasper, another old friend from St. Louis. I hope you don't mind if I bathe and dress and leave my bags here."

"No, of course not." But I really didn't know what I wanted. Holy Mary Mother of God, as my Rolfer used to say, when he hit a tender spot.

I told him I had to go. "Just pull the back door shut when you leave, please."

And I left. I didn't discuss the reservations we had for dinner. I couldn't. I was too worked up. I'd feel better when I went about my day and he went about his. We would come together later and talk about our separate days over a nice dinner at Bix.

I walked up the hill to my car. Relieved to be alone, I sat in the driver's seat, thinking about the bill at Zuni. He really didn't get it. We came from such different places, I told myself. And then I recalled something that Nan Grand-Jean had said. Her response to my proud declaration about never dating businessmen: "And how has that worked out for you?"

I'd never actually had to think about my independence. I'd always had it. I knew people made compromises in relationships. But jeez. I rolled the window down. I took in the cool winter air.

I connected the white earbuds to my new iPhone from Robert and dialed Steve Grand Jean. I had half an hour before I had to head downtown to my meeting.

"Hi, how did things go?" he asked. "I've been waiting to hear."

"It was all over the place," I said, with a deep sigh. "I left him at my house in a chair with a pile of newspapers at his feet. He was just sitting there, and I had to go," I added. "I felt as if I were coming unspooled."

"You did? Why? What happened?"

"Well, he's great, everything about him is, but he's kind of crazy, wild. I am interested, definitely interested,"

I said, rolling the window down further. "But he's out of control—shaken one minute about Bonnie, kissing me the next. He doesn't get that romance must simmer. It's all too much too soon. He's generous and funny. But what shape is he in physically? And I am not so sure about his mental state. He speaks to two therapists and he's just taken himself off of what they prescribed since he feels so good," I said all in one breath.

"Well, he's excited," Steve said. "You are the first happiness that's come along since Bonnie got sick five years ago. He's been through the wringer. Did he actually do anything wrong?"

"No, not really. He's just never been out on a date. Never spent a night at a woman's house. He isn't exactly healthy. I mean he's a walking recipe for a heart attack."

Steve had no chance to respond before I continued.

"Did you know he arrived like the Cal Marching Band in the middle of the night with an armload of presents? Really extravagant presents. But he's a manly man, the real thing, I give him that. And I love his lack of self-consciousness."

Steve was meeting Robert for lunch at noon. "Let me talk to him, suggest he slow down a bit. He's a great man

Peggy, and he was a fantastic husband, don't forget. He's one of the most creative businessmen I've known," Steve explained. "He's been filled with anguish for so long, he probably doesn't know what to do with you. As for being overweight, that's what can happen to former athletes like him who were extremely active when young. They get older and don't stay as active, but their appetites do."

"I really don't know how to handle this, and I'm not expecting you to do it for me," I said. "But we can't keep it up at this pace. We need a little space, a little common sense. I'm going to be tied up for a few hours now. I'll check in with you later. And hey, thanks, Steve."

I got off the phone and called Barbara as I was driving downtown.

I'd only had a bite of muffin to eat all morning and was running on fumes.

"Barbara. I feel so weird. This is all too much," I said.

"Calm down, Peggy," Barbara said. "Last thing we were worried about was how your jeans fit. It's all going to be fine. He's great. He's funny, gentlemanly, and smart," she enthused. "He's easy to talk to, and he's a man who knows sports. And he sure is in love with you."

I told her he couldn't be. "How could he know so

soon?" I explained that I didn't have my usual arsenal of arguments against him. He wasn't a rogue; he was honest, polished, and full of life. He'd been very successful and hadn't come off a bad marriage. He was good on so many levels… "But I've got to breathe." I told her.

Barbara offered to call Robert and feel him out, tell him they all liked meeting him and see if he'd settled down a bit.

I gave her his cell number and told her that Steve was going to talk to him, too. I suggested she wait, since I wouldn't be able to talk to her again for a couple of hours. I'd call her when I was done with Slow Food.

It was a relief to feel I could rely on Barbara and Steve to talk to Robert. But why did I need stand-ins as if we were all in junior high? Why couldn't I talk to him myself? Because he didn't listen.

I went into the Slow Food meeting, happy to have a different focus for a while, but I couldn't really concentrate on the plans for the Labor Day event at the Taste Pavilion at Fort Mason, where I'd been asked to preside over the California Olive Oil Pavilion.

At about four, when the meeting was finished, I quickly said my goodbyes and went to call Steve. The news wasn't very good. He'd tried to reason with Robert over lunch, told him he'd sort of scared me by trying to move too fast and being too insistent. He also told Robert that I was concerned about his being out of shape. "I'm afraid he didn't take it very well," Steve said. "He was so high when we sat down and I think he was quite deflated by the time lunch was over. He said he was going over to Wilkes to do a little shopping, to make himself feel better."

Instead of waiting to hear from me, Barbara called to say she had also talked to Robert and had been briskly told that he didn't need more advice. "He knows you were overwhelmed," Barbara said. Well, I guess he was too. He sounded pretty wounded, poor guy."

"Poor guy? What about me? What about his romantic bombardment?" But now we were both really worried that his feelings were hurt. "Maybe I've been too rash," I said. "I'd better get home and talk to him."

Barbara told me he might not be there. When she'd spoken to him an hour ago, he'd sounded as if he was going to take off. "I don't stay where I am not wanted," he'd told her in no uncertain terms. And she'd said to him that it might not be a bad idea.

I raced home, parked, and tore into the house. Marina

Montenegro, my longtime housekeeper, was there because it was Friday—her day to be there. "What happened?" I asked. "Where is he?"

"I met him, and then he went upstairs. He came down right away, dragging bags of clothes, with shoes and shirts hanging out. He was in a hurry," she said.

"You mean he left?" I asked. "Did he leave a note or anything?"

I didn't wait for an answer. I dashed up the stairs. I went into the spare room where he'd left his things and found nothing but a forlorn piece of rumpled paper lying on the bed.

"Too bad it didn't work out.
Robert."

CHAPTER TEN

R OBERT'S NOTE KNOCKED THE WIND out of me. But shocked as I was to find him gone, his departure showed me he had backbone. There was only so much he could take of my being unreceptive and impatient. "Good for him," I said to myself. But that was just my first reaction. Had I finally met *the* man? And now it was over just like that?

I didn't know what to do with myself. Scream, cry, hit a pillow, eat a Butterfinger? I did what I always did—got on the phone. I needed my friends, the ones who had been in on the romance from the beginning. My first call was to Cal. She'd known me the longest.

"Don't be silly," she said. "This is just the beginning. You have not heard the end of Robert Fisher."

That was also Christopher's opinion, so I allowed a bit

of hope to bubble up.

I left a long message for Annie Lamott, who would have made me laugh at myself or come up with a brilliant spiritual solution after the many years of unfortunate affairs and growing sober that we'd shared. But she was away.

Finally, it came down to being on my own. After all, I was 63. I lit a fire in the living room and sank into my orange leather chair. The same chair Robert had sat in for a little too long that very morning. I tried to blame him for misunderstanding me—blame was sometimes my first reaction. But I was longing to call him and say it didn't have to end—we just needed a breather.

I sat there watching the fire, trying to talk myself down off the ledge. Finally, I felt I had to take some action, so in a fit of characteristic impulsiveness, I texted him, apologizing for having asked Steve and Barbara to deliver my message, rather than talking to him myself. "I'm sorry you left," I found myself writing, and pushed the Send button. But how sorry was I? I immediately wondered, since I still felt the solution I wanted had to be on my terms. Meanwhile, my phone was lying dead as a doornail on my lap. I waited some more but didn't hear a word.

Why had finding myself the object of Robert's out-of-control passion been so disturbing? What threw me, I realized, was my fear that it might not turn into love. But there was no doubt that Robert knew what love was. He'd known for 50-odd years. I'd never been with a man for more than three or four. I reminded myself that I'd been consistently attracted to men with a certain pretext of unavailability, a disdain for devotion. Never had I chosen a man with whom I could imagine growing old. That idea hadn't even occurred to me by my 50s.

I'd been hoping my days of judgment were over. Did I really care at this point if Robert was a little bit out of shape? No, not really. But I'd resisted letting myself accept him because he was so unlike the men I usually ended up with. For years I'd veered away from guys like him because I didn't think we'd have enough in common. I'd never tested the waters. And now I'd driven him away and lost what could have been my best chance yet.

Over dinner at Zuni, he'd told me he knew by the look in my eyes that he was not what I was expecting. And he was absolutely right. I hadn't expected to meet such a fully formed man, a put-together human being, someone I perceived as straight. He'd been so funny and playful on the phone and in our emails that I hadn't been prepared for his seriousness, his intensity, or his disconcerting straightforwardness. I'd needed him to be a tiny bit enigmatic, to keep me wondering. Or did I mean, I needed him to torture me a little because I'd always mistaken torture for love? Had it taken him leaving to make me realize this?

All this rethinking was making me weary. I broke down the fire, turned off the downstairs lights, and headed up to bed. As I climbed the stairs, I had one more flash. I was now beginning to understand the way my treatment of Robert reflected the new Peggy Knickerbocker I had become. I could let him go if it didn't seem right.

The next morning was bright and windy, with whitecaps on the bay. A day full of promise. I woke up determined to write Robert Fisher one more time.

Dear Robert,

It was sad here last night. I could smell your scent upstairs. It was as if our romance had not developed slowly enough for us to discover one another—boom, boom, boom. Hard to accept how great you said I was, how much you loved me, how much you wanted me to marry you. I couldn't allow it in or believe it because you couldn't possibly have known me well enough. We hadn't created enough space to get to know one another. You didn't know my shortcomings.

I complain, but these are the things that caused yesterday's breakdown.

It's not that I'm by any means an expert, but I think a healthy romance has to have some give and take, some play, a pause, as well as a bit of mystery. Did you really see me, or did you just see a woman who fit the bill as you'd written it, except for point eight, about my age? Did I really see the man you are?

I'm going to say it right to your face; you are a seductive man. You made me open up, even in the epistolary stage. You obviously know how to have a successful union. You retired to take care of Bonnie. Most men wouldn't have done that. I admired your inclination. I know you now want to live. Your emotions are beautiful and raw.

And then, as for my concerns about health, believe me, I know I am far from a perfect specimen—I am almost through middle age, but I am vigorous and healthy. I try. My spiritual life follows. It is vital for me to be with a man who is mindful of some of the things I take seriously—health—mental and physical. I don't want to fall for you and then see you follow in your father's footsteps by having a heart attack and leaving me a widow.

I'm a normal California woman, I watch what I eat, and I love to exercise. I've had eating issues myself. It was my job as a food writer to be obsessed with food, and I still am. You are fantastic as you are, but would I be completely out of line to mention vegetables?

I am not sure it will work, but if we were to want to give it a fighting chance, we both would have to make adjustments. I am willing, within reason—are you? I would try to be less defended. What adjustments do you think we'd need to consider, both of us?

I am sorry I didn't get into some of this with you yesterday. I lacked the guts. I didn't have the words. I am only capable of opening up at my own pace.

What do you say?

Love, Peggy

In accordance with our pattern of email synchronicity, Robert's message came while I was writing mine.

Dear Peggy .....I have no computer hook up .....just my phone.....I am truly sorry about yesterday ...I made some bad choices .....starting with leaving, but Barbara thought leaving was a good choice, as did I...I really don't know what happened, but I have my opinions....you went from planning a trip to LA next week to having Barbara and Steve deliver a strong message to me...I don't like having messages delivered except by the person with the message...

I think you tried to grow fond of me but couldn't get there physically or emotionally so you continued to say I was moving too fast ...I felt it was a slap in the face...deny your own participation,

but there is no doubt I led the way...I take responsibility...I made one comment about being a lucky man, and you said it made you uncomfortable...I suspect there was more going on for you...I meant everything I said and stand by it. I think you had a fundamental change of heart and didn't know how to get out of it, so you got Barbara and Steve to tell me that you were very upset ...I could only show you that you had total control by leaving...

I apologize, but it is probably a relief I am out of your life ...I love you so much that I can't bear to see you upset ...I'll just go away ...I want to give you time, but I don't think I can please you, and smothering you with affection, nauseates you .....

I am truly sorry I brought you so much discomfort...hope you keep the presents or give them to charity...I doubt you want to try again, but if you do, I would love the opportunity to improve... maybe we can both be better...but if you just can't warm up to me, let's move on...I can take N...I can't take anything but the truth...

I am so sad and sorry, but I will survive...you must be relieved and feeling peaceful ...Robert

I went to the farmers' market after reading this. I was happy he hadn't given up. I remember gliding through the rows of stalls. Even the stinging nettles and parsnips looked lovely.

By the time I got home, he'd already started texting.

In fact, we texted back and forth for a good part of the day, acting more like kids than fumbling old farts. I was at my desk, Robert was on the beach in Carmel, sitting by a cypress tree. We talked and wrote. We got over the craziness of the previous week and began to move ahead. We made promises, pledged compromises, came to an agreement about issues we'd skirted. I would try to be more open. Robert would try to make himself healthier. He'd cool his jets.

We decided I'd fly down to LA the following weekend. Just to cover my bases, I said I might stay with my dear friends Mary and Bob Estrin who lived close to Robert. In fact, the two houses were near enough that Mary and I could have passed Robert and Bonnie on the mountain trails we all hiked on some of my visits. Over the course of the day, Robert and I made plans for what we'd do. We talked about whether his daughter Jackie and her husband Scott would join us for dinner.

"My daughter Carrie will barely speak to me," Robert said. "She is not alone in thinking I am crazy and disrespectful to Bonnie's memory." He wished his children, including his son Cass, who lived in Florida, were not upset with him. "They just don't understand.

They think I am behaving irrationally. I probably shouldn't have told Bonnie's mother, nearing 100 and totally with it, about you."

"Robert, it's only been three months since Bonnie's death," I reminded him. "It would be hard for me if I were in their place. Right now, they are so tender, so filled with grief and they probably want you with them." I understood that his family's concerns had nothing to do with me. They were just worried that their dad and son-in-law was going off the deep end.

Then I became obsessed with planning the perfect weekend. Of course, I was determined to have us eat great food, so Robert left the choice of restaurants mostly up to me. I knew I ought to follow his lead. But I have very close friends in LA, some since childhood. I always saw them when I visited. My mother called me Madame Full-Charge when I got crazy planning too much, trying to fit everything plus one into a short period of time.

We spent a good part of the following week on the phone, combing through our past histories. It was a period of intense unearthing. I held some things back, but I told him more about my years of hard work and discovery in North Beach. I also told him stories about how Flicka and

I had conducted our catering business and restaurants by the skin of our teeth.

By the time I packed and drove to the airport, Robert was beginning to get an idea of the unconventional life I'd led. I let him know it didn't seem at all that unconventional to me. While I regretted the parts of my life that had caused me to waste time, I wanted him to accept that I was the woman he'd fallen for because of the risks I'd taken and the experiences I'd exposed myself to. I hoped he fully understood what a crazy and unlikely romance we had gotten ourselves into.

CHAPTER ELEVEN

M Y FLIGHT TO L.A. took the usual one hour, but it seemed to last forever. The second the wheels of the plane hit the runway, I turned on my phone. "Landed," I texted Robert. As I descended the escalator to baggage claim, I saw him—my big, amorous, shaven-headed man, holding up one of those chauffeur's signs for incoming passengers. In bold letters, it said, "MADAME FULL CHARGE, Welcome to LA." I felt a little embarrassed until he flung it down and gave me a reassuring hug. Then everything snapped into place. He was happy even waiting for my luggage. And his sense of humor was growing on me.

I suggested that the first stop on our itinerary could be an organic hotdog stand in Culver City called *Let's Be Frank*—the guiding motto for this phase of our

relationship. I knew that grass-fed hot dogs, or any kind of hot dog, would be Robert's cup of tea, despite his previous determination to immediately take me to a posh LA spot. At my behest, Sue Moore, the owner whom I'd known in San Francisco for ages, made him an extra special one, adding her own stash of pickled onions. He was about to order another when I decided to do something that had been weighing on my mind and ask him about a present he'd given me in San Francisco that I'd brought along in my suitcase. "Would your feelings be hurt if I wanted to go look at some other orange scarves? I loved that you got me such an extravagant present and orange is one of my favorite colors. I just thought another design might suit me better."

Robert's feelings weren't hurt at all. Instead, he was pleased that I hadn't been afraid to tell him the truth. "It's the first building block of a good relationship," he told me. "I like it when you talk like that." So, he took me to the Hermès shop in Beverly Hills where we found an orange scarf with palm trees and lions and leopards that we both thought was perfect for me and made the exchange. It was the first errand we did together. I remember taking note of that.

"Where do you want to go next?" he asked. We could have gone straight to his house, but I wasn't quite ready for that, and maybe neither was he. I wanted us to be together a few more hours before we took on all that history. "Let's go to the new Getty Museum," I proposed. It was an unusually clear day for Los Angeles—a good day to see the gardens—especially my favorite, the cactus garden. And I'd read about a show of photographs by Graciela Iturbide, whose work I'd admired. This time her subjects were the women of Juchitan, a town in Oaxaca in Southern Mexico run by a formidable matriarchy. I'd featured them in a story I'd written for Saveur about Oaxaca years ago. Robert and I were fascinated by their headdresses—long braids interwoven with ribbons and flowers and some of the most influential women had been posed with iguanas on top of their heads. It was just before dusk when we left there, having racked up another successful first—a trip to a museum.

Twenty minutes later, however, as Robert drove up a long road past a country club toward a gatehouse, I began to feel a little anxious. What would it be like entering the house where Robert had lived with Bonnie for two decades? I could already feel my defenses going up, judging by my critical objections to the manicured suburban landscape. At the gate, a guard in a brown uniform nearly fell off his stool trying to get a look at me. "Hello, Mr. Fisher. How are you this afternoon?" Robert told me the guard had been very kind to Bonnie during her illness.

What was I doing in a gated community? It felt so over-protected here, so removed from society, from the Los Angeles I knew. Why had a liberal, compassionate, art-collecting couple chosen to live behind gates when they'd been so close to Santa Monica, with its charming houses near the beach? But that was me—Santa Monica was where I might have lived. Robert opened my car door and carried my suitcase up to the house.

Pots of soft red geraniums lined the three broad tiled steps leading up to its entrance. The house was big and broad and attractive in a vaguely Mediterranean way, just like all the other houses around it, give or take a few thousand square feet. Leaf blowers made their irritating racket—the surround sound of suburbia. Where were the people, the kids playing, dogs running around? Everyone was inside, outside there was not one hint of life. Robert opened the front door without using a key.

The vestibule had soaring ceilings and great light. I

peered into an immaculate living room that looked as if it was never used, with buttery beige leather armchairs. It felt as if the furniture had just stopped whispering. The heart of the house was the family room. Comfortable black leather chairs and a sofa were clearly the ideal choices for grandchildren and the leaps and bounds of four dogs. Function ruled here rather than form. I wanted to come back and read the titles of the books that lined the walls on either side of the fireplace.

Robert led me out to the patio, which was green and lush and had a rose garden at its center, hemmed in by gardenia bushes, with splashes of blue hydrangeas. He pointed out the towering redwood he'd planted twenty-three years earlier, which he said was a symbol of longevity. The house had been built on high ground. I gazed out over a sparkly view of downtown L.A. while Robert went inside to prepare to show me his and Bonnie's art collection, which required some fiddling with dimmers and light switches, since he wanted everything to look just so. It gave me a moment to catch my breath and absorb my impressions. This was an expansive LA house, overflowing with a certain neat and organized charm.

With Robert about to show me the art collection, I

felt we were coming to a critical moment. He had been looking forward to sharing something that was dear to him, but what if I didn't care much for what I saw? How could I keep my judgmental self from saying something that might bring him down, hurt his feelings? I knew a little about the Southern California artists he and Bonnie had chosen to buy. This could be the point where some woman in my shoes might ask herself, "What if he has black velvet paintings?" In fact, I'd known a Los Angeles artist, Peter Alexander, who painted on black velvet, but did so in a masterful way.

I waited for a few minutes as the sky began to darken, for the moment when Robert would ask me to come into the house. It turned out that I loved most of the collection. Nothing was showy, but you could tell that every piece had been thoughtfully selected. The art was abstract, colorful, and mostly large in scale. Yes, there were some Peter Alexanders but not the black velvet ones. A number of the artists were people I knew slightly. There were works by Laddie Dill and Robert Graham among others. I knew a good collection when I saw one. I added art to the interests Robert and I already had in common.

He had gone to the flower mart earlier with Paige

Doumani, the woman who'd wanted him to go out on one date before meeting me. They'd filled the rooms with spring flowers—irises, tulips, and fruit blossoms. I knew he'd done his best to make the house welcome me so that I would feel at ease in it. In the dining room, a huge wooden bowl that he had filled with green apples rested on a handsome dark oval table. I sat down for a few moments on one of the black-leather chairs, and was surprised by its comfort. Cabinets held gigantic wine glasses. Dozens of them in varied shapes for different types of wine. The wine glasses in my house were just one size fits all.

Robert took me into the kitchen, where he handed me a box I'd sent to myself. It contained the bottles of olive oil and red wine vinegar I'd picked out just in case his kitchen lacked the things I felt essential to my well-being and gastronomic happiness. If there was nothing wonderful to eat at his house, I'd thought, we could just add a nice hunk of Parmigiano-Reggiano and some lettuce, or pasta. But I also thought, I'd lived alone for too long. I was set in my ways.

As I put the bottles away, I spotted one of my favorite oils, Laudemio Frescobaldi on one of Robert's shelves. I'd recommended it in my book on olive oil back in 1997.

Why had I not given Robert more credit? Even most people I knew in the food world didn't have Laudemio Frescobaldi oil in their kitchens. When I asked Robert how he'd heard about it, he explained he'd met the Italian wine and olive oil family, the Frescobaldis, on a business trip to Florence. He loved the way certain foods tasted with the oil drizzled on top.

So, the flowers were beautiful, the art was exceptional, the oil was top-notch, the house was easy, and Robert was a doll. He took two delicate wine glasses down from the cabinet and poured us cool drinks of San Pellegrino. We toasted one another. And then it was time to meet the dogs.

Robert opened a door to their quarters in the back of the house and in they came, wiggling and squealing and happy to see us. Darlin', the English bulldog, and Cosmo, the wire-haired dachshund, came right for me. I got down on the floor and roughhoused with them. Darlin's big creased ugly face pressed close to mine. I thought of my father's stories about the bulldogs he'd had in his childhood. And little Cosmo's brown eyes were so dark they seemed to be rimmed with kohl. When he tilted his head, his beseeching gaze broke my heart. He was the smallest and oldest one—his muzzle all gray. I picked him up, but he wiggled out of my arms, as if to say, "Not quite so soon." The other two were more interested in dinner. Baby, a tough little well-nourished French bulldog, eyed me with skepticism, while Lilly, the petit basset, after shyly looking me over, went for Robert, the dispenser of food and love. We had to feed them in four separate spots, so they wouldn't get possessive and squabble.

As they ate, Robert took me to see the upstairs and unpack. By now I'd forgotten the Victorian idea I'd had about staying with my friends, the Estrins, nearby. I was sure Mary and Bob would understand.

Everything was going well, with none of the mania of the preceding week. Maybe Robert was better on his own turf. He touched my shoulder softly as we got to the second-floor landing. It made me shiver in the best way. I thought to myself, this is the start of something big.

CHAPTER TWELVE

THE MASTER BEDROOM WAS THE best-looking room in the house, with sandy brown walls and white plantation shutters. Piles of white pillows leaned against the carved wooden headboard of the tall and generous bed. Two old appealing Parisian club chairs sat on either side of the fireplace opposite. I could have spent all day in this room, if it hadn't been for the portrait of Bonnie looming, larger than life over the mantel. Damn it, she was beautiful—soft, kind, and lovely looking. I'd wanted her to have a big hairdo and a stretched-out face. Then I could have found fault with her, but really, she was the opposite. I sat down in one of the chairs, her eyes upon me. It was odd, but for some reason, Robert had made me feel that even though he'd had one of the all-star marriages, he was now completely with me in the present moment. I was struck by how right everything felt. Later I learned that Cass, Robert's son had called the housekeeper, Rosa to ask if his mother's portrait had remained in place.

I walked into the adjoining bathroom, which was bigger than my bedroom, and then into a walk-in closet, bigger than my bathroom. Robert's daughters had moved Bonnie's clothes out of the house, so Robert's took up all the space—his clothes could have filled a small-town men's store. Nothing about his clothing was small-town, though, or even small. A rack of belts hung on the door. When I counted them later, the total came to 126. The guy was out of control. Suits, jackets, jeez, the wardrobe of a businessman, organized by color and then shade. And the shoes! My attraction to shoes paled compared to the array that was carefully polished and stored with shoe trees on their shelves. I tried not to let my jaw drop.

Cosmo, who had followed us upstairs, paraded back and forth beneath Robert's crisply laundered shirts, scratching his little sausage back on the starched cuffs and shirttails. I was clearly falling for the two males in the house.

I hung up a few things, leaving my suitcase open on

the floor as I took a shower and started getting changed to go out for dinner. Baby, the Frenchie, grabbed my bra and dragged it across the carpet, tormenting Cosmo.

Cosmo picked up the bait. I chased them into the bedroom, bare-ass naked, Bonnie's eyes still upon me, as I tried to get the bra from them. They tugged and growled and teased. I was a little scared they might bite me. Then Cosmo let go and the bra smacked Baby in the face. No real harm done, except to Baby's pride. For me, there was a soggy bra.

We went to A.O.C., a French Mediterranean spot, for dinner. The chef was a favorite of mine—cooking with a light hand. The food was simple and fresh, with great flavors. A.O.C had been my choice, and while I found it excellent, I discovered that Robert was not a fan of small plates. He didn't like to share food, preferring Midwestern-size helpings of his own. But he'd rise from his chair when I left the table, and to seat me upon my return. His manners were every bit as good as my father's.

When we got home, not wanting to call it a night, we took his dogs for a walk. As we strolled with them, the atmosphere of the community was still—earthquake-still, as is said around here on certain balmy days. The only sounds came from misdirected sprinklers leaking onto sidewalks. Not one other person was out enjoying the quiet night. I was reminded of the scenes in Robert Bechtle's paintings that are often streetscapes bereft of human existence. I could imagine how lonely it must have been for Robert here, after Bonnie's death.

When we got home and got ready for bed, there were her soft eyes again, saying, "I'm looking at you." I asked Robert to turn out the lights. We were both feeling a little shy in this new setting. But that didn't last for terribly long.

The next day was sunny and warm, not unlike the other three hundred sunny days a year in Los Angeles. We went downstairs and took our second cups of coffee into the garden. The dogs followed. They napped on the warm tiles as we talked the hours away. He told me more about his children and grandchildren. I told him about the two restaurants I'd run with Flicka McGurrin, whom I'd known, along with Cal, since the second grade. Wearing a short white nightshirt and happy my legs weren't going unnoticed, I walked around the tidy, protected garden, deadheading a few leaves and flowers. I was feeling totally at peace. I still wasn't ready to speak of love, but I could feel I was on my way.

Robert needed to talk about Bonnie, and I was glad to listen. I admired him for making no apologies about getting teary. The way he let his guard down seemed valiant to me; most men would have hidden their pain. As he showed me some more albums of their past few years together, he started to sob. He sobbed and sobbed. I put my arm around him and just stood there with him. I thought that maybe we really did have a chance at success, since at least one of us knew how deep love could be.

Robert had made reservations that evening at one of his favorite spots in Santa Monica. We were going to meet the Doumanis. Despite all the flowers Paige Doumani and Robert had bought to greet my arrival, I couldn't help wondering how she and her husband Michael were going to feel about me, given how close they'd been to Bonnie and how Robert had turned to them for advice on this new phase of his life. After some thought, I chose a casual outfit I would have worn on a Saturday night in San Francisco: high heels, a hot pink shirt, and a shortish multicolored striped skirt.

Michael, who like Robert was in the L.A. financial world, was handsome and suave—a man's man, who enjoyed golfing and playing cards at his club. His mother, from what Robert had told me, had been an unusual woman. She would cook elaborate Lebanese dinners for her sons and their wives and friends and then slip away after the last course to play poker in all-night games in sketchy neighborhoods. Michael's wife Paige was not cut from the same cloth, but she was elegant and charming and very kind to me. She appeared in the restaurant dressed all in black—not edgy black, but a reserved feminine outfit that set off her blond shoulder-length hair. We found common ground when she told me about her Italian garden and her garden club; we discovered that we admired the same landscape architects and we both loved cats.

It also turned out that I knew Michael's brother Carl, who lived in the Napa Valley and had started the Stag's Leap winery just when I was getting my foothold in the food world.

Although the Doumanis hardly had to convince me that Robert was an unusual person, they made it a point to praise his acumen in business and his extraordinary devotion to Bonnie. Finally, Robert, who seemed to have memorized some of my anecdotes, changed the subject to my unconventional life in North Beach, giving me an opening to tell them about the restaurant I'd run in the 1970s.

As I sat there sipping sparkling water and listening to their interested reactions, I felt quite comfortable, though the thought did come into my mind that I had somehow landed at the grownups' table. I had a subversive urge, which I suppressed, to be naughty.

There was a strange moment when I got up from the table and almost found myself saying, "May I be excused?" as if I had been sitting with three people from another generation. When I went into the bathroom, I took a look at myself in the mirror. "Would you rather be home in San Francisco or here with Robert and his nice friends on this proper double date?" I decided I would rather be right where I was, even though a tiny bit of me wanted to shake up the safe, privileged world Robert and the Doumani's represented to me that night. As it turned out, I grew to be very fond of the Doumanis.

The following morning an unexpected chance came to introduce Robert to another of my own dear friends when I got an early call from Susan Andrews. She had been part of my life since the early 1970s when she and her husband dropped in at Mooney's Irish Pub in North Beach, where I was running my first restaurant with Flicka.

Susan told me she wanted to fly down that day to have

dinner with Robert and me. "I feel, as your close friend, that I must meet him. I cannot live through another disaster with you."

I turned to Robert, who had already heard all about Susan, and told him her plan.

"Of course," he said. "I'll grill a steak and you can make a Caesar salad. When is she coming?"

Later that day, as I was checking things out in the kitchen, I was struck by what a good cook Bonnie must have been. She had excellent equipment and a carefully assembled drawer of baking gear. Suddenly I felt almost as if I knew her. Her cookbooks included some of my favorites by Paula Wolfert, Alice Waters, and Marion Cunningham. Everything was adding up to a woman who probably would have been a kindred spirit.

But when I opened the food cupboards, I found nothing but processed foods. Robert had done the shopping during the years of Bonnie's illness. He'd cooked for the rotating nurses that filed through the house, and for Bonnie and himself. I was looking at brand upon brand of barbecue sauce, pancake mixes, salad dressings, canned corn, soups, and fruits. I'd been so immersed in the Northern California food scene, the organic, local, seasonal routine that I couldn't help myself. I lacked all humor and tolerance.

I grabbed a couple of heavy green garbage bags from under the sink and flung myself up onto the counter. Shelf by shelf, I swept all of it into the bags to be given away.

Robert came into the kitchen, catching me in the middle of my wordless rant, my banishment of all that food. Since he was too astonished to say anything, I did some fast talking, hoping I hadn't gone too far.

"You don't mind, do you? My only excuse is, we agreed to eat healthfully." I immediately suggested that we go straight to the Brentwood Farmers' Market and load up on alternative choices. Later, I overheard him proudly telling a friend who had phoned him that there wasn't one can left in the house, not a bit of processed food. I apparently could do no wrong.

At the market, we filled the trunk of his car with lettuces, cheeses, good organic beef, olives and almonds, and tangerines for dessert. Back at the house, we had fun preparing for the simple dinner. Robert set up a bottle of wine for Susan. He told me he didn't know how he was going to marinate the meat because all of his sauces were gone. "How about good old salt and pepper and a splash of olive oil?" I suggested. "The meat's excellent, it will stand on its own." He said, "You're the professional, might as well give it a try." I couldn't believe how easygoing he was.

Susan arrived in the late afternoon. I cringed when the guard called with her name. Oh gosh, I'm busted. I'm falling for a man who lives in a gated community. San Francisco doesn't have gated communities.

Kind woman that she was, Susan didn't mention the gatekeeper—she grew up in Los Angeles. She was a nicer person than I. In she came and started a tête-à-tête with Robert that didn't stop until 8:00 p.m. I picked up snippets of conversation about politics, education, and eating meat, as I made the salad, set the table, and lit the candles. She followed Robert out to the grill, where they became so rapt in conversation that he burned the meat and half a tree. He used so much lighter fluid he singed the hair on his arms. "Peggy is going to laugh at this," Susan told him, "she's a bit of a purist and doesn't believe in lighting fluid."

Fortunately, some of the beef was salvageable, and the talk over dinner was a delight. Susan told Robert all about growing up in LA with her movie-star father— Dana Andrews. We discussed child-raising, Susan's husband Buddy Rhodes, concrete artisan extraordinaire.

By then I felt pretty sure she wasn't putting Robert into the disaster category.

When she was ready to go, she and Robert hugged, both of them looking wet-eyed. It had been quite a first meeting. They'd connected as I figured Robert was used to doing. When I walked Susan out to her rental car, I hardly needed to ask how the evening had gone. She has never been one to spare words. She turned to me, grabbed my shoulders, looked me in the eye, and said, "He's your guy, Peg, behave yourself."

Chapter Thirteen

BY THE TIME ROBERT CAME BACK to San Francisco a couple of weekends later, more of my friends were clamoring to meet him. Susan Andrews, who was now his ambassador, got a table at our favorite pizza place in the Mission District, Delfina. Our lively and opinionated group included Valerie Velardi, my neighbor and yoga teacher; Davia Nelson, a Kitchen Sister on NPR radio; and Tony Oltranti, partner of Bob, the pianist who had serenaded us at Zuni with Valentine songs.

The mood was upbeat, since Susan had already circulated positive reports after her trip to visit us in LA, everyone expected the gathering to be what she called a "friendly inquisition." Nobody knew quite how to begin, so Robert started the ball rolling. He asked my friends how each of them had met me, and what their first impression had been.

Valerie recalled running into me, probably in the early '80s at a comedy club in San Francisco where her then-husband was performing. We found that both of us laughed at exactly the same jokes and had friends in common. She told Robert that we'd seen each other through some difficult times a few years later when we both were living in Paris.

Susan spoke of how freely and candidly we'd talked to each other, back in the 1970s, about mutual friends the first time we met in North Beach. She'd shown up at Mooney's Irish Pub, wearing exactly the same long black, flowery Foxy Lady dress as mine that night. It laced from the belly up to the breast, showing a fair amount of skin. "We've shared a certain *élan vital*," she told Robert. "A zest for life," she explained when he shot her a quizzical look.

"Just how zesty?" he asked her. The gang at the table generally agreed that I'd always had a way of getting every last drop out of life—of a bottle, a meal, or a man.

Before Robert could ask any more questions, Tony Oltranti spoke up. "When I was first meeting Bob's friends about ten years ago, Peggy was particularly friendly to me and made me feel comfortable."

"And today," he announced, "we're all here to find

out if you'll be a good match for Peggy." His tone was lighthearted. What he wanted to know was whether Robert planned to take me away to Los Angeles.

Robert assured him that he wasn't going to ask me to do anything I didn't want to do.

Davia was specifically interested in hearing about the music Robert liked. He admitted without the least embarrassment that except for Diana Krall, Ella, and most Black female jazz vocalists, he and I did not have similar favorites. "In fact, early on, Peggy told me that the presence of Celine Dion and John Denver on my iPod were grounds for not moving forward."

She just laughed.

Susan interrupted to say that she could attest to Robert's politics. Not only was he unquestionably liberal, she was sure he'd move further to the left as a result of being exposed to life in the Bay Area.

"I did ask Peggy to marry me, as I think you all know," Robert put in, laying all his cards on the table.

"I hear you did that right on a LA freeway even before you met her," teased Tony. "We just don't want her doing anything rash."

"You call that rash?" Robert said. "Anyway, my offer

remains there until she's ready."

I had been enjoying all this good-humored banter, to which I hadn't contributed a word, and was surprised when Tony apologized for having sounded like part of a firing squad. But I could see that Robert was up for the challenge, even though there really hadn't been one. I loved Robert for his total lack of pretentiousness and his approachability.

The mood around the table had changed now that the ice had melted. Since they were starting to feel that Robert was going to be one of us, my friends threw caution to the winds and started teasing me about some of my more outrageous past slips of judgment.

"What about that Frenchman who had the opened bottle of Scotch on his coffee table one Christmas night as you sat together looking out at the Eiffel Tower?"

"And those colorful artists from the Art Institute?"

"And remember that Hungarian you met in Mexico?"

As the laughter died down, Susan turned to Robert. "You do know whom you are dealing with? I was so relieved," she added, "when Peggy finally got sober and started writing."

She went on to say that she no longer worried about

me the way she did a couple of decades ago. To illustrate her point, she brought up the notorious boyfriend who was a drug addict. "Of course, none of us had ever known a serious addict, that we knew of."

Feeling a little anxious by this time, I glanced at Robert, trying to read his expression while reminding myself that he'd already heard some of my history and seemed to enjoy the details. But I hoped Susan would zip it up on the man in question. She didn't know how innocent Robert was.

Unfortunately, she was just getting started on this particularly embarrassing story. How I'd finally figured out the nature of this guy's problem and politely told him to leave my apartment. How later that same hot day after she and I had gone to the beach and she'd driven me home and we'd climbed the stairs to my apartment, we'd found that my front door had been kicked wide open and was hanging on a hinge. Next, we discovered that my jewelry box and a case of my grandmother's silver was gone, as well as the keys to a convertible I'd rented. "That was when Peggy realized she'd been had."

Everyone chuckled weakly, except Robert. I felt a rush of shame slither over me. All this had happened forty-odd years ago but the humiliation of it suddenly felt fresh.

I adored Susan, but there were some things I'd wanted Robert to hear about from me.

On the drive home, as Robert and Valerie chatted, it dawned on me that wherever we went in San Francisco we were likely to bump into people who'd have *their* own tales to tell about me.

Once we were alone in the car, I noticed a gloomy expression on Robert's face. "Was that a little too much information for you?" I asked him.

He sounded put-off and came right out about what was bothering him. "Does everybody in San Francisco know about your past? Does everyone think you were wild?"

"Robert," I said as we parked, "you and I grew up in separate universes." I went on to say that as he knew very well from what I'd already told him, I hadn't exactly spent summer nights on the back porch listening to baseball and licking frozen custard cones. And that what would have seemed wild in St. Louis was child's play in San Francisco. And no, I didn't think everyone thought I was wild. "I had a lot of fun and I liked my image as I grew older, or so I told myself."

We walked into the house and continued the discussion as we sat down in the living room. Robert didn't seem to care that I'd taken drugs. He focused only on the number of men in my life. I told him what a boy-crazy teenager I'd been as a result of going to an all-girls school. But that I wasn't about to divulge more memories when he seemed so disapproving.

I thought about how insecure I'd always felt as a teenager about whether or not I was attractive—a problem I traced back to my being told I was fat by my father. I'd loved the attention from boys, and later the men I went out with to prove that my father was wrong. But really no amount of reassurance, I thought ruefully, had been proof enough.

Robert, on the other hand, had never experienced being a young bachelor in a rowdy town; he'd never been a bachelor. Considering the age I was now, weren't his concerns about my past irrelevant? Here I was worrying about my sagging rear-end—which he thankfully hadn't noticed—and he was thinking about me as a twenty-two-year-old.

"I had a great big life that got me where I am now," I told him. "And I have become, by the way, the woman you have fallen in love with."

I wanted him to understand how much my life had

changed at forty when I started writing and got into recovery. But he seemed to think I had lived my entire adult life horizontally.

I started talking about what I had accomplished, about the catering business Flicka and I had built up. "We did Francis Coppola's 40th birthday party for thousands," I told him. "We were in demand. We even opened a branch in LA and got music and film industry jobs."

"Did you cater for your parents' friends?" Robert asked, as if that would make us legit. I recalled a dinner at a fancy house before a big opening of the Gertrude Stein collection at the museum. Flicka and I had used Alice B. Toklas's recipes including her famous hashish brownies—minus the hashish, I told Robert. That, I silently remembered, we'd saved for ourselves. "We even did a lunch for Nancy Reagan that we almost didn't pull off because our waiters refused to serve her.

Robert agreed that I hadn't just wasted my youth, but then he wandered back into murky water and returned to the subject of how many men I had slept with.

Trying to maintain my calm, I tried to explain that North Beach had been filled with temptation for an impressionable twenty-something divorcée. I'd never lived among poets, musicians, and artists, people so unimpressed with social agendas. Everything had seemed new and exhilarating to Flicka and me. Before North Beach, we'd led quite privileged and sheltered lives; we'd been debutantes. With our longing for adventure, we'd been seduced by the world of the Beatniks, before it disappeared.

Robert started trying to convince me his life had been far from conventional. "I was hardly a Boy Scout, Peggy." His wildness had consisted of drinking too much at times. When questioned, however, he admitted he'd never had a hangover and only had one hit of marijuana in his entire life. Everybody thought he was outrageous for his appetites, but he always worked hard to support his family and took his work seriously.

"Well me too," I barked. "I had to, I was on my own."

He didn't think that was the same.

This made me furious. Did he think I'd ever been supported by any of the men I was with after my marriage ended? Didn't he get that I'd always earned my own living?

Robert couldn't seem to understand why I hadn't wanted to lead a mainstream life. He floored me by demanding, "Did you have no sense of saving yourself for the right man?"

"Oh, for God's sake, no," I said, "The thought never occurred to me. But I was always sure whatever relationship I was in would last."

The air cleared when he decided to share a racy San Francisco story of his own. During the 1970s while I was running around North Beach, he'd come to the city on a business trip and gone to a party in Sausalito given by a friend from St. Louis. He'd walked in wearing a business suit and immediately realized that he was overdressed because most of the guests were half-naked and writhing around on the floor, smoking marijuana.

"And what did you do in your suit?" I couldn't resist asking him.

"I left," he said.

I assured him it wouldn't have been my scene, either.

But then he got back to what he called my lascivious past. He was maniacal about this subject.

"No," I yelled. "We are done. It wasn't lascivious to me!"

I woke up beside him the next morning unable to see how our differences were going to be resolved. I called my brother Tony and told him I had no intention of defending my past to Robert for the rest of my life.

Tony reminded me that for someone who hadn't been in San Francisco during that time, it might be hard to imagine all the things that had been going on. "Don't talk too much about it, Peg. Give the guy a break and let him get to know you as you are today."

CHAPTER FOURTEEN

B Y THE TIME ROBERT RETURNED TO LA, we'd agreed to live with our differences. Of course, he would have preferred me to be a 63-year-old virgin, but I knew I wouldn't be as fascinating to him if I were. As for me, I was sorry he hadn't done more exploration of the wild side so that he'd have a better understanding of my earlier life. Even its vernacular was unfamiliar to him. When someone said, for instance, that a person was "out there," Robert wasn't clear about what it meant. One day he asked me what "camp" meant. Sometimes I felt as if I were translating for a foreigner. But we couldn't alter the different ways we'd lived our pasts, and out of our mutual sense of exasperation came a timid truce. We agreed that an acceptance of our earlier lives would come with time.

In every other way, we were yielding to each other at a comfortable pace. When I'd tell Robert that I was going upstairs to read on my bed, or that I was off to have coffee with a friend, he no longer took it personally. He clearly got along well with everyone and he'd fallen completely in love with my house. "It's the country inn I always wished I'd owned," he'd say. He took over unloading the dishwasher and always put gas in the car. I found that his energy matched mine. We both loved to get going early in the morning after he'd read the *New York Times* and the *SF Chronicle*. Writing emails to various columnists about city politics or sports when he thought they'd got it wrong made him feel like a San Franciscan. He couldn't go to bed unless he'd sent off a thank-you email for a dinner we'd just been to.

During this period of duking it out, we both knew that something formidable was bubbling up, and that made it possible for us to remain resolute. The spark and the chemistry were there even if the details were not quite nailed down. The bottom line was that we truly cared about each other. Our differences would matter less as we moved along.

I was relieved that Robert's ardent devotion had

tempered—that he had become able to see me realistically. The kind of romantic fascination he first had for me could have laid a flimsy foundation. I had to be sure that he could accept my shortcomings, my past, my feisty moods, and restless anxiety. I saw him now as he was and understood his powers. I listened as he talked on the phone counseling various young people in business. Fascinated by leadership, he spoke with disdain of toxic leaders. He brought creative solutions to business challenges.

I'd been totally naïve about corporate life and most business issues, apart from what I'd learned as a small business co-owner. I would certainly never have made a good corporate wife when I was younger or now, so it was lucky I found Robert at the late moment I did. Earlier, my judgmental nature would have led me to make certain assumptions about what being with Robert would entail— that his colleagues were bound to be boring, that I would have to wear St. John suits with pantyhose to dinners, that I wouldn't be allowed to speak my mind or, worse, might not have enough to say. And, would anyone in Robert's world have been interested in what I had accomplished?

His readiness to accept me as I was, allowed me to take little comforting risks around the house. I knew he wouldn't wince if I ran downstairs bare ass naked to the laundry room to get a warm nightgown out of the dryer. Around other men, I'd been more modest, but since Robert always had a good word to say about any exposed part of my 63-year-old body, I dropped the towel. I felt comfortable about him coming in to chat while I soaked in the tub with my shower cap on.

He expounded to friends about how he intended to compress his life when he got back to L.A. "Living in this house," he'd say, "is like living in a submarine." He was going to start scaling down his clothes, shoes, art collection, wine glasses—all with an eye to moving in with me. I had no garage, no space to store extra detergent or his compendium of shaving products. But he was pleased I kept a case of good olive oil on hand.

I was happy to see that he was following my lead in taking better care of himself. He would probably always be a big guy, and by now I thought he looked good just as he was. Unlike other men who needed to constantly be in control, he was open to any reasonable suggestion I made. He now ate blueberries and yogurt for breakfast. He loved my salads and was surprised when I made something like a parsnip purée actually taste good. If I suggested we go to Marin County to take a walk, he'd grab his hat, always hoping an outing would include a good meal. If I told him I'd discovered a little café that served St. Louis-style breakfasts, he'd be out the door and warming the engine. Sometimes I asked myself, was it all coming together a little too neatly?

His estrangement from his family remained an issue.

After his two weeks with me in San Francisco, he returned to LA, determined to make peace with his daughters and their families. They still were disturbed by their father's rush into a new relationship with a stranger, and I really couldn't blame them. They probably felt abandoned by Robert just when they needed him most.

Jackie was the more willing not to pass judgment on our relationship, yet she too was still experiencing excruciating grief. I was sure the two young women were unnerved by the idea of their father gallivanting around Northern California, meeting new friends, and having great experiences.

Meanwhile, I still hadn't told him I loved him, though there were moments when I just about did. A lingering fear preoccupied me—repeating the failures of my past. During one of our daily phone conversations, I found myself saying,

"Robert, I feel closer to you in just a few weeks than with any man since my first marriage." He was heartened that I'd spoken so warmly to him, but I knew it didn't do much to ease the pain and guilt he felt about his kids.

The weekend Robert would be flying back to San Francisco from L.A. was my brother Tony's birthday and we were invited to Calistoga to celebrate. When I asked Robert if he was ready to be introduced to the entire Knickerbocker family of seven, he said he couldn't wait. "What should I bring as a birthday present?" he asked me over the phone. "You are the clothes horse," I joked, "you won't have any trouble finding the right thing. Just don't buy him a book on fly fishing, everyone always does."

I was already feeling romantic as I drove to the airport to pick Robert up. I'd even fantasized about greeting him with the old naked-under-a-fur coat trick, but aside from the fact that it was quite warm, and I didn't own a fur coat, we would be traveling in broad daylight and needed to beat the traffic to Napa. Practicality ruled in late middle age. Still, as he descended the escalator carrying a silver box that must have had Tony's present in it, I felt a rush of excitement.

The weather was sensational that day. We sailed

through the city and across the Golden Gate, missing most of the traffic. As we drove deeper into the Napa Valley, the landscape made Robert go into a swoon. It shimmered yellow—bright mustard was blooming between the rows of vines. Robert had always been drawn to that part of Northern California, for its wine, its lore, and his business. He had visited it often during the past forty years and pointed out some of the wineries he'd stopped at. Even though Robert's drinking had ceased years ago, he still enjoyed talking about wine, and his knowledge of the subject was deep.

I told him a bit about my nephew Keary who lived in Portland with his family and about my two twenty-something nieces, Ferren and Molly, and how I'd loved to spoil them when they were younger by taking them for manicures, to R rated movies, such as *Purple Rain*, and up and down escalators, which didn't exist in the Napa Valley.

It was dusk by the time we arrived in Calistoga. We dropped our bags and showered at our hotel before driving up the hill to Tony's house, where every available bed was taken by his kids.

We were greeted by an enthusiastic band of Knickerbockers. Molly and Ferren, immediately, took

Robert over, stationing themselves on either side of him and exuding such warmth that he had to remove his sweater. As they led us into their house, Mary and Tony gave him the once over. Meanwhile, Robert was smiling, shaking hands right and left, ready to get to know everyone. His big, warm, confident personality instantly made a good impression on my family. Before long, my great-niece, four-year-old, red-haired Amelia, who had arrived earlier with her parents Keary and Francesca, insisted on performing a dance of her own choreography for Robert.

After leading the applause, he took a stool at the counter facing the kitchen, his purple and white polka dot socks flashing under his soft dark brown suede shoes. Since my brother had a thing for shoes, too, Robert's didn't go unnoticed. Meanwhile, the spicy aromas of Tony's vegetable tagine were making everyone hungry.

When we sat down for dinner, Robert raised his water glass and made a toast, "Four months ago I thought I'd never find joy again. My wife of 44 years had died. Thank you for bringing me into your family, Peggy, and I appreciate all of you for including me," he said in a still unsteady voice. "Happy Birthday to another phenomenal cook in the family."

Tony and I had chosen careers in food, I suppose

because our mother had been such a good cook; her festive meals were positive memories for us. When we wanted to spend time with her, it had usually been in the kitchen. I had taken up cooking rather haphazardly just because I loved doing it, not because I felt it was my *métier*.

My only background was a credential to teach French at the secondary level. Tony had pursued cooking with a more formal approach, working at Domaine Chandon in Napa and then going on to *stage* in Épernay at Moët Chandon, really studying French cooking, while I learned by trial and error.

Both of us had opened restaurants and run catering businesses. I'd worked mostly in the city with Flicka, while he chose the wine country. Our ongoing conversation about food had started in the 1960s when we were just kids. We still had conversations about what we were making for dinner, and what had just come into season in Tony's organic garden. My brother kept bees, canned produce, and made preserves. He was a farmer, and I reaped the benefits.

During Tony's first marriage, we didn't get together much. Family gatherings were sometimes strained. But when he got divorced in 2003 and a couple of years later married Mary, our relationship became close again. Now we talked at least three times a week, if not more, spent holidays together, and I loved to go hiking with him, Mary, and her dog.

Robert gave Tony a lovely sweater the color of the peacock-blue ink that I used to use in eighth grade. I wondered how Tony would handle the thank you. He was a man of the country, and of subtle army greens and tans. Robert, sensing the color might be off, told Tony he could always exchange it if it didn't suit him. Tony told him he loved the sweater, but another color might look better on him.

"Oh, I can count on you Knickerbockers for telling the truth about color," said Robert, remembering that I'd wanted to exchange the scarf he'd given me.

The evening ended early on a high note with everyone walking us to our car. We made plans to hike with the family the next morning.

"Wow, you and them too!" Robert said as we drove down the hill. "Your parents must have done something awfully right. *I love your family.*"

The next morning Tony and Mary met us at the hotel. The hills on the hotel's property were lush after early March rains. The sun shone through the dense oak and fir forest. The trail was soft with leaves, the inclines gentle. As the four of us walked together, suddenly I heard Robert say, "Tony, would you hang back with me for a minute?" and I saw them slowing down.

"I have a proposal to discuss with you." Tony told him not to worry, that he already knew what was coming. "Well," I heard Robert ask him, "what do you say?"

By this time Mary and I had slowed down and couldn't help eavesdropping. "I'm glad to finally get the old girl off my hands, Robert, "I heard my brother say. "I have never seen Peggy as happy, and I have been through a lot with her. If Peggy wants to marry you, you have my blessings."

After the hike, when we were having Arnold Palmers on the screened-in porch of the hotel, joined by the kids, Tony proposed a toast. "Robert has asked me for Peggy's hand, and I told him we all would be delighted." I was surprised by how emotional and shaky I felt hearing my little brother's announcement, and was amazed that it had all been put forth as if it were a fait accompli.

I felt a little ridiculous. I hadn't said yes yet. I hadn't even said I loved him. Why was I still holding back? I asked myself. I knew Robert Fisher was the man for me. And each day I knew him, I trusted him more. It was myself that I didn't trust. Would I be a good partner? Could I sustain a long relationship? Could I finally settle down to being with someone day in and day out?

My nieces hit me on the shoulder and gave me their thumbs-ups. I knew how excited everyone was for me as I sat, trying to look demure but a bit sweaty. For decades, I'd stood alone. Now, if I could only say yes, I could have a great partner by my side to celebrate the big moments of our lives.

CHAPTER FIFTEEN

I FELT A DEEP CONNECTION TO ROBERT on the drive home from Calistoga through the Napa Valley. A light fog had rolled in over the vines and mustard flowers. Their greens and yellows became a splashy blur.

I remember what I cooked that night—a blue cheese soufflé and a green salad. As I whipped the egg whites, I felt as sure as I'd ever feel about Robert. My senses were alert as I worked in my kitchen, my focus clear. I knew exactly how to proceed. Before bed, I would tell Robert Fisher I loved him.

We climbed into bed soon after dinner to read the paper. When it came time to turn out the lights, Robert sat on his side of the bed. The moon was almost full, making the water gleam. I felt so relaxed and drowsy I could barely keep my eyes open. He leaned over to kiss me goodnight,

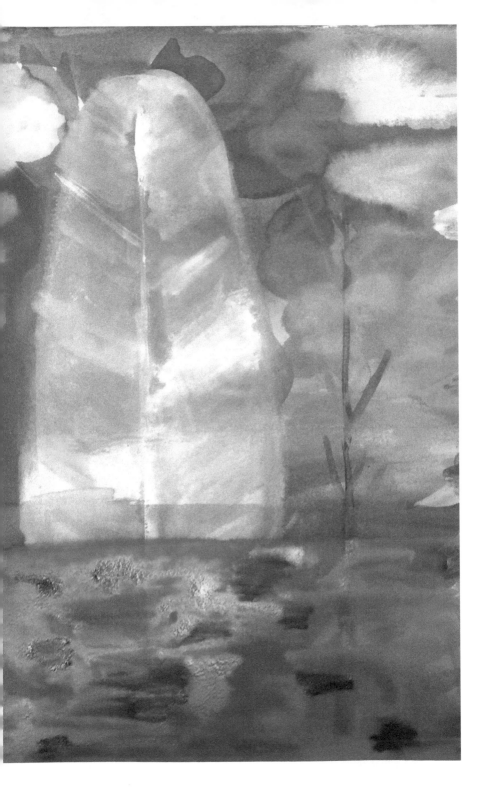

and whispered, "I love you, Peggy Knickerbocker."

Gone to the world, I mumbled, "I love you, too, Robert Schneider." Then I closed my eyes, happy I'd finally said it.

"ROBERT SCHNEIDER! WHO THE FUCK IS ROBERT SCHNEIDER?" he shouted. He stood up, very agitated, then slumped back down on the bed, forlorn.

Wide-awake, I sat up in bed, trying to make sense of what had happened. "I have no idea why I said that. I don't know where that came from."

"You mean, you don't know Robert Schneider? I think you better act fast to explain this one." Falling dead silent, he stared me down.

Meanwhile, words had started pouring out of me, anything I could think of. "Robert Schneider is an old, old friend. He was Flicka's and my first chef at Pier 23 back in the mid-80s. On the day of his interview, he wore glasses with pale blue frames, just like mine, and a black and white herringbone overcoat, also like mine," I knew I was sputtering, but I didn't want to stop until I'd made everything clear.

"I wanted to hire him on the spot. He prepared a meal for us and I loved his French-California style of cooking."

"Yes, Peggy," Robert impatiently interrupted me. "But why did you invoke his name at our most significant romantic moment?"

"It's just what I told you. Robert Schneider and I are old colleagues and friends, that's all."

"Well, that's very nice, but it doesn't explain why you said, 'I love you, Robert Schneider.'"

"I happened to think of him when I was making the soufflé. I know this will just get me in deeper, but the last soufflé I made was for him, a few months ago. That's why he must have flashed into my mind."

"Peggy, this is just getting worse and worse," Robert fired back. "Oh, I forgot to mention one important thing. He's gay. Really, Robert, he has never been a romantic interest."

Even this didn't satisfy Robert. "Haven't you told me that some of your gay friends have had children with the women to whom they were formerly married?"

How on earth did he come up with that? I wondered, although it was certainly true. Hints of his jealousy had erupted earlier but not like this. I didn't like it one bit, but that was not the problem on the front burner. It was me.

"Robert Schneider has never been married to a

woman; he's only attracted to men. He and I are dear, dear friends. You'd like him too. He loves dogs."

My ears were ringing. We had to settle down before this went further south. I kept trying to make him see that it had only been a crazy slip of the tongue.

"Give me some time. This is how I process things," Robert finally said before we went to sleep. But I knew from his tone that he wasn't going to drop the subject. And he didn't. He was starchy stiff with me the next morning. I faltered but gave up. I couldn't make him trust me.

A night or two later, we drove over to Oakland for the long-awaited opening of Camino, a restaurant owned by a young couple I knew. It was a grand affair, with great open fires burning in pits at the rear of the restaurant. Legs of lamb and sausages dangled on strings above the flames. Robert, lover of restaurants, was excited to be there.

The first person to greet us was Gilbert Pilgrim, who co-owned Zuni Café, the restaurant we'd gone to on our first date, on Valentine's Day. Gilbert was such a dashing man—head to toe in Hermès, worn in his own way, and his gray hair pulled back into a bun at the nape of his neck.

"Gilbert," I said proudly, "I want you to meet Robert Schneider." Oh shit, I'd done it again. I could feel myself flushing bright red from head to toe.

"Hi Robert, "said Gilbert, "we've already heard a lot about you. Word moves fast in cooking circles. Peggy and I traveled around China together, so I know her quite well."

"Actually, Gilbert, Peggy apparently doesn't know me very well, because she keeps forgetting that my name is Robert Fisher, not Schneider. But whoever I am," he said, putting out his hand. "I am happy to meet you, too."

The party was gathering momentum. The moment Gilbert moved on, Robert asked me, "Did you travel alone with Gilbert in China?"

"Oh, I know where this is going," I said wearily. "Yes, we were together for a few days before meeting our friends. But don't get any ideas about Gilbert. He has a very nice husband."

"This is crazy, Peggy," Robert whispered through his teeth. "You know I'm open-minded. But while you are introducing me as Robert Schneider, you tell me you traveled all over China with the handsomest man in the room."

"I don't know what to tell you anymore. Robert Schneider just keeps coming out of my mouth. And Robert, you are going to have to have a big heart along with your open mind."

"I do," he insisted. "I do have a big heart. Just try calling me by my name, and things will get much better very fast." Suddenly we both started laughing and he put his arm around me, and I planted a big one on his cheek.

That night we sampled marvelous food from great brimming bowls and platters: herby lamb ribs, spicy sausages, stewed beans, and tasty greens. We also ran into a lot of people I knew, and once or twice I mistakenly introduced them to Robert Schneider because now that name had lodged in my subconscious and I simply couldn't stop doing it.

We were walking out of Camino, completely stuffed, when Robert and I almost had another disagreement. "What do you have in mind for dinner, Peggy?" he asked me.

"Dinner!" I said. "What do you mean, dinner? Didn't we just eat our body weight in amazing food?"

"Well yes, but I like to have a proper dinner—to sit down, order, and talk. Those were just hors d'oeuvres."

I held back an answer that would have sounded quite sharp and considered a diversionary tactic. Knowing how much Robert liked sweets, I suggested we head over to Berkeley to Ici a stunning, little sweets shop that Marie

Antoinette would have frequented if she had been alive and living in the Bay Area. One of its specialties was a delicate ice cream sandwich made with ginger snaps and Meyer lemon ice cream. Robert-whatever-his-last-name-was loved the idea. He ordered two.   We   drove back to San Francisco, joking about Robert Schneider. I told him my embarrassing mistake would just add another laugh to his version of our romantic story, next time he told it.

As we approached the tollbooths at the Bay Bridge, I was ready to say exactly what I'd originally intended: "Robert, I love you. Robert Fisher, I love you."

CHAPTER SIXTEEN

I ONCE HEARD A STORY about a mother octopus putting her baby to bed. She got all the tentacles neatly tucked in, and then tiptoed to the door. She heard a rustling. A tentacle had emerged. She returned to tuck it in, then another came out from under the covers, then another, and so on. That was the way it was with Robert and me. Just when I'd finally said, "I love you," Robert pressed me harder about marriage.

I told him I thought it would be a good idea for us to live between our houses for a while, as we got used to living together. But he wanted action and a commitment right away.

I made an appointment with my therapist whom I saw only intermittently. He suggested we wait a year. If we were still drawn to each other for all the right reasons, then marriage would be the reward for our patience.

When I got home that day, I told Robert that my therapist had reminded me that if I'd waited a year to let my last boyfriend move in, enormous pain would have been averted.

"Well, I'm hardly in a league with your last boyfriend, but okay," he said, "we'll wait." He, too, had started thinking maybe we should wait a year to be fair to his children and Bonnie's family. But he didn't look happy.

"You do want to get married after a year, don't you?" he asked me. "Because I like being married. I'm good at it. And I want to be married to you."

"It's not that I consider marriage bourgeois," I tried to explain. "I just don't feel passionate about it as you do. I think it's great that we love each other. I just don't want to mess that up."

We seemed to be on the verge of another huge discussion, but Robert cut it short by lowering the boom. "I think you need to consider this very seriously, Peggy. As much as I love you, I will move on if you don't want to get married."

That completely threw me. Really? I couldn't believe he could be so black and white. I felt the drums beating,

I knew how scared I was that marriage to him might be something I wouldn't be able to pull off.

Would I become impatient, grow bored, or not be able to compromise? That had been my pattern in my first marriage and the relationships that followed. Then I reminded myself how well I'd done on my own, during the years before I met Robert, how I'd regained confidence in myself. If I wanted to marry Robert, I could pull it off, I began to feel. I certainly couldn't imagine losing him at this point. That would be unthinkable.

"I said, "if it means that much to you, I'll marry you. But I'm keeping my goddamn name."

"Keep it, Peggy," Robert said as he put his arm around me. "Maybe I should take on yours," he said, half-seriously. "Call myself Robert Knickerbocker Fisher, this being San Francisco. I'm glad we'll have a year to call each other fiancé. I never told you, but I really hated being called your boyfriend."

I felt dazed by the speed at which I'd been steered into complete agreement. Yes, I'd said I'd marry him, but that didn't erase my doubts.

My biggest concern was that it was only four months since Bonnie's death. Why couldn't Robert wait for everyone to adjust before making plans? Why were he and his children at such different levels of grief and mourning? I was unprepared for what followed when I asked him that question.

He just let go and burst into tears. His sorrow was profound and although I longed to comfort him, I knew enough not to interfere. No words from me or anyone would have helped, so I just stood behind him kissing the top of his head until he let out a deep sigh and stopped.

"The grieving process is never the same for all within a family," he said as he sniffled and grabbed his handkerchief. He explained that in one shocking afternoon Bonnie had gone from having a sharp pain in her stomach to being sent to Acute Medical Services at UCLA Hospital. From there she went from getting an MRI, to a brain CT scan, to being told she had kidney cancer which had metastasized all over her body, along with a catastrophic tumor on her brain. "During the course of one day, our lives changed forever," Robert said.

Over the next few years, Bonnie would suffer through ten operations and all sorts of medical atrocities. To care for her himself, Robert stopped working. "I never wanted another person in the house to steal our privacy," he explained. But he felt he had lost Bonnie long before she died.

Eventually, he became so exhausted; he'd had to hire nurses. He also was helped enormously by his children and friends.

"I started grieving that first afternoon in the examination room when we realized something terrible was wrong and I grieved relentlessly for four and a half years, and I am still grieving," he told me.

I felt like crying too, because Robert's sadness was so heavy. After dealing with my mother's stroke and my father's Alzheimer's, I could imagine what he'd gone through. Tony and I had been torn apart by the suffering of our parents, and then our stepparents.

I told Robert about the day our family sprinkled our stepmother Marti's ashes up the coast. I couldn't imagine my life without her. Her unconditional love replaced my sorrow at never quite feeling it from my blood parents. And so, I felt miserably alone that day until I got a call from my darling Niloufer King. A longtime friend, she rang to say she'd like to play a piece of music on the piano for me. When I arrived, she led me upstairs to her bright-yellow music room. There, surrounded by books and Oceanic artifacts collected by her husband, she had me lie on her brown leather sofa and proceeded to play Schumann's Romanze. I let go and cried and cried until I looked over at Ordle, her green parrot, perched on her head, keeping time. And then, as if that gesture was not enough, she served me lobster salad with papadams.

After his sorrow was spent, I suggested to Robert that we go outside for some fresh air. We took a walk up my hill to get ice cream cones. That actually helped, a lot. We took the long way home and remained quiet.

Once we got back to the house Robert said to me "I want to let go of some of the pain for now. That cry did me good, but it will always be there. It's time to look ahead."

Then he said, "Let's set a date for our wedding. How about Valentine's Day 2009?"

"Robert…" was all I could think of saying for a few moments. Then, "I guess you're ready to move ahead."

Over the next few days, we started making practical decisions. First, we had to think about our two houses. Since the country was in recession, selling either mine or Robert's would be a tough proposition.

For me, the big draw to living in Los Angeles was my Southern California friends. But then I thought of the stultifying smog, the horrendous traffic—all too much for a Northern California girl. How could I leave my own family, my San Francisco friends, the food, the farmers' market, the Dolphin Club, the culture, the beauty? The world I'd lived in all my life? I was a third-generation San Franciscan, for God's sake.

Fortunately, Robert fully realized how delightful it was to live on Hyde Street. The more time he spent in Northern California, the more he embraced the life, so the idea of his staying gradually became a fait accompli. He was particularly seduced by my ritual gatherings with friends, most of which focused on food.

He had become very fond of my friend Cal, partly because she'd been the one who brought us together along with Steve Grand-Jean. Robert enthusiastically joined a group of us when we went to Cal's and her sister Patty's old family ranch in Sonoma to make balsamic vinegar. Robert got to help harvest and crush the grapes that provided the must—the sweet, reduced juice that becomes the vinegar. When the feast that followed included homemade pasta with the chanterelles that some of us had gathered from under the oak trees on the ranch, he was over the moon.

Back home, he joked that when he had been troubled

by an event in the news, he wanted me to call Flicka to go for a walk. She always had an opinion that he loved hearing. He grew fond of her grown children who loved him back.

Robert was "living the life" to borrow a favorite expression of Christopher Hirsheimer's. After she started Saveur magazine with her colleagues, Dorothy Kalins and Colman Andrews, she would remind me that I was living the life in California that they were trying to recreate in a skyscraper in New York City. By that Christopher meant a life that was simple and earthy, filled with great friendships and the best food.

And for decades, Robert had been reading about Northern California life in Sunset, Saveur, and Gourmet, the very magazines I wrote for. He might have even read some of my articles. Now he was devouring that life.

Few of our friends discussed the stock market at the dinner parties we went to. The exception was another childhood pal Dick Thieriot, the former publisher of the San Francisco Chronicle. One night, Dick appeared wearing an orange tie with tiny bulls on it. When I tried to get a closer look, he said I probably wouldn't understand the implication. Robert got a good laugh out of that.

Then one weekend Dick and his wife Angie invited us to go duck hunting with a group of friends. Neither of us would be shooting. Instead, we admired the landscape along the eastern bank of the Sacramento River where we picnicked. That day we saw five bald eagles, a flock of pheasants, and streams of ducks blackening the sky. The caviar, marrow on toast, and foie gras Angie served that night was pretty memorable too. (Everything but wild duck, which she couldn't stomach.)

"You have made me a more complete man by asking me to come to San Francisco," Robert told me. When I asked him what he meant, he gave me a list of the important new experiences he'd had in addition to meeting all my friends.

He now flossed and used an electric toothbrush. He had switched to using Apple products and was beginning to like eating figs, rhubarb, and beets. Instead of wearing handsome business suits, he now found it perfectly normal to wear pants from the Sports Basement that zipped off at the knee.

I told him he'd changed me too but in less obvious ways. I was convinced that being in love had made me more agreeable to most people. Stubborn old Peggy had softened, become less selfish and impatient, and I had to admit I liked having him around.

At first, I'd worried that some of my gay friends were not so sure about Robert and assumed I'd now be less available to them. Then one of them, Steven Barclay, my confidant in Paris and California, wrote me a reassuring email saying it was hard to share me, but he and our mutual friends were becoming happy that I'd found Robert.

Soon after Steven's email, my landscape architect friend, Nancy Leszczynski, came to visit from Italy, dying, of course, to meet Robert. She and I'd been single pals in San Francisco in the early '90s and had remained close. I invited her and a group of her old friends to dinner. Among them were the women who owned Cowgirl Creamery—Sue Conley and Peg Smith and their partners, Nan Haynes and Cheryl Dobbs. They'd given me the cheese I'd served to Robert when he first came to Hyde Street in the middle of the night.

We were all raising a glass to Nancy when Peg said, "And I would like to toast Robert whom I suspect has never sat across the table from four lesbians."

And, without missing a beat, Robert responded by raising his glass and saying, "No, Peg. I have not and I look forward to doing so many times in the years to come." That was my Robbie—a man who had no gay friends in LA and now had a dozen, all of whom he kissed on the lips.

In San Francisco, everything was moving ahead beautifully, but in Los Angeles, things were still unresolved. Robert's daughters were upset all over again by the prospect of their father living so far away.

I knew a little about Jackie from our one dinner back in February but nothing about Carrie. I still hadn't met her. There was the possibility that she would never change her mind. She still found Robert's behavior reprehensible. She missed her mother and was angry with her dad for not being more thoughtful. "Pissed at you, Dad, not at Peggy." I started reading books on the stepmother role and talked to friends who'd become second wives and lived through these challenging periods. I had my own late stepmother, Marti, whom I could use as a role model for doing a fine job. Carrie's reaction was apparently quite normal, I discovered. In fact, I understood how she felt.

Jackie had been willing to meet me, and when Robert asked her to have dinner with us the first weekend I came to LA, she and her husband Scott had agreed. Robert thought they were probably curious and wanted to make a welcoming gesture. "She always does the right thing," he said.

Robert had proudly told me what a little ball of fire Jackie was as a girl. "She was a great swimmer. I can still see her brown body propelling herself at high speed through the water like an eggbeater."

I'd been so eager to make a good first impression, I kept changing my mind about what to wear, finally choosing a crinkly gray silk blouse with a stand-up collar, a black skirt, and heels that were a little too high to walk in gracefully as a 63-year old.

The moment we walked into the restaurant I could tell that Jackie had had her hair and nails done. That had immediately put me at ease. I'd realized Jackie also wanted to make a good impression. I told her how I'd ransacked my closet and admitted that for days I'd been a little on edge about meeting her.

We'd ended up laughing about our mutual anxiety. Jackie had made it easy for me at that first dinner by being talkative and warm. But I knew that seeing her father with a new woman couldn't have been easy.

She told me about her three kids—her daughter Ellie,

and her two boys, Joey and Sammy. I couldn't wait to meet them, I said, hoping I wasn't being presumptuous.

Jackie said that Ellie, the oldest, was the one who'd been most affected by Bonnie's death. I was relieved she'd found a gentle way to bring up Bonnie. There was no way we could leave her out of the conversation. I told her I was terribly sorry she'd lost her mother and asked her how she was coping.

Jackie startled me by saying bluntly, "Every single minute is insufferable."

When I told her I'd lost my own mother when I was thirty, she let me know that she felt there was no right way to talk about death. She looked as if she might need to cry.

Quickly pulling herself together, she ordered some hors d'oeuvres for the table. "See, what did I tell you, Peggy, Jackie takes care of everything," Robert said. He must have felt it was time to change the subject.

By the time the platter of cheeses and cured meats had arrived, Jackie, Scott, and I were having a spirited conversation about our favorite TV programs with the Sopranos on the top of our lists. Robert didn't join in because he only watched the news, sports, and Masterpiece Theater—nothing scary or bloody for him. But he listened as we all chatted, and I could feel his relief.

Jackie told me she was more of a reader than a TV-watcher and our similar tastes in books gave us a lot to talk about, without grasping for other safe subjects. We'd both loved Muriel Barbery's The Elegance of the Hedgehog and found Cormac McCarthy's The Road the heaviest, darkest book we'd read. Maybe we'd be discovering other books together.

Jackie obviously adored Robert and had fun teasing him. "Daaaad," she would say whenever he went on about something too long.

"Has Dad told you yet about his closet collapses?" she asked me. "You've seen his huge stuffed closet, his fancy room filled with clothes and shoes, haven't you?" Well, of course, I had.

"We all have addictive personalities in our family," Jackie went on. "Dad is addicted to buying clothes. A couple of times he jammed so many onto the hanging poles and the shelves that the closets came unscrewed from the walls and crashed to the floor."

I wasn't surprised.

"Dad loves fancy," she told me. And I'd felt the

beginnings of acceptance when she added, "Have you noticed that, Peggy? Fancy everything. You'll see."

"There we were," I remember saying to Robert as we drove home from that dinner. "All adults; glad to have met, glad it was over."

CHAPTER SEVENTEEN

L ATE WINTER BECAME EARLY SPRING without a hint of change in the LA air. But in San Francisco, where it was colder, we could feel the transition to the next season—our first spring together. I started swimming in the Bay as the water warmed a bit.

We were meeting more of each other's friends and understanding ourselves better as a result. Robert had as many as I did, which I found unusual for a man. His contagious enthusiasm was often a feature of the amusing stories they told about him. As I became more and more comfortable with Robert, I found his house in LA more agreeable.

We'd started driving down to do some packing and measure the rugs and furniture that we wanted to bring to San Francisco. We filled the back of my Mini with clothing and small paintings and sculptures each time we drove north. Time flew by on those six-hour trips. We loved each other's company.

When May rolled around, Carrie was still not ready to meet me and apparently didn't feel great about seeing her father either.

It was killing Robert. He told me that although Carrie was a lot like her mother, her stubborn streak was just like his.

I was willing to wait for Carrie to come around, but Robert wasn't. He wanted to make something happen, stir it up. Patience was not revealing itself as one of his virtues. He told me his kids had always thought his behavior was hotheaded, and in a way, I agreed. One of his friends called him Passion-fish, and really it could have been his middle name.

I tried to imagine how Tony and I would have felt if we hadn't already known our mother's friend Marti when my father fell for her after our mother's death. Marti and my mother had gone to UC Berkeley together and remained close. We not only knew Marti, we loved her and hoped she would agree to marry our father. But it would probably have been different if he'd brought a stranger to meet us.

As we grew tighter as a couple during the next three months, Robert put it out there that we were aching to be with his kids and grandchildren. He was gaining some insight into his over-the-top behavior and was trying not to be Maximum Bob, his other nickname, reminding me from time to time that he was still an all-or-nothing guy. By now, he understood that he mustn't pressure Carrie. Instead, he called Jackie and asked her to come over for lunch one Friday in May when we were spending the week at his house.

I was eager to prepare something especially delicious for my second meeting with Jackie, but my plans got foiled when I got lost going to the market. I ended up buying some prepared salads because I realized that by the time I got home, she would just be arriving.

Jackie didn't seem to mind eating takeout food and told me I'd have other opportunities to cook for her. I took that as a positive signal. But after we ate our curried chicken salads in Bonnie's kitchen, I got the feeling it would be good to leave her alone with her father for a while. When I came back in, I saw they were sharing a hidden stash of chocolate chips. I put my hand out and joined them.

Clouds were rolling in overhead so the three of us

decided it wouldn't be too hot to take a walk in the canyon in the middle of the day. My favorite dog, little Cosmo, the dachshund, came along. He'd followed Bonnie everywhere and now he followed me. I hoped Jackie didn't notice.

That day she had seen me in her mother's domain for the very first time and I'd felt a certain amount of heaviness in the air. As I served lunch, I'd been conscious of being in Bonnie's kitchen, serving food on her plates, putting her silver on the table. I was sure Jackie was wondering what would happen to her mother's things when Robert gave up the house.

Before this became a divisive issue, I wanted to let her know that there was nothing to worry about, because I intended to do exactly what Marti, my own stepmother had done after my father died, and this cool afternoon seemed as good a time as any to gently spell that out. There was no graceful way to open up the subject, so when the three of us were out on the trail pausing to admire the view, I plunged right in. "There's something I need to say, Jackie. Whether we want to or not, we're going to have to talk about the way our lives are going to move forward, and it's going to be awkward, I admit it."

Robert had been somewhat prepared for us to have this

conversation, but I could see that Jackie was completely taken by surprise. "I agree," she said after a moment of silence. "It is all pretty uncomfortable and new."

I told Jackie that Marti had been the best teacher I could have had to prepare me for the situation I found myself in now. "My father," I explained, "just like your dad, decided to remarry only a year after my mother died. I told Jackie what Marti had done for my family. How she and my father had had a few very good years even though he was in the early, undiagnosed stages of Alzheimer's. Since he could barely add and subtract, something no one outside the family knew, she had taken over the finances that had been in a shambles since my mother's stroke. When my father died, it had been Marti who'd sorted everything out and divided up the small inheritance he'd left us. There was not one moment of confusion for us," I told Jackie. "With Marti, we always knew where we stood."

By then we were walking on the trail single file and I could almost see her lower her shoulders as if she felt a sudden relief.

"Peggy doesn't need anything, Jackie," Robert blurted out. "She and I have about the same amount of money and we want everything to be clear to you and Carrie and

Cass." He pointed out that we wouldn't be taking much. "Peggy's house is half the size of Mom's and mine."

"And I have all the possessions I need," I added.

Jackie was looking a little embarrassed. "Thanks, Dad," she murmured. "I think I get it."

But now that we had jumped into this conversation, there was more for her to know, and I wanted Carrie and Cass to know it too. "When the time comes for us to move, I will photograph the items we will take with us. There'll also be a list: a dining room table, books, a couple of French leather club chairs, tables, good Oriental rugs, and art."

"Lots of art." Robert had jumped in. "Everything else will be up to you three to split."

I felt we'd done a noble job with a difficult subject and that we could put it to rest for now.

The following morning Carrie called Robert, inviting us over for Mother's Day. She'd evidently talked to Jackie. Besides Mothers' Day, it was also her younger son Jeremy's fourth birthday. "I was beginning to wonder if I would ever hear from Carrie," Robert said.

May 11, 2008 was bright and warm, and I knew it was going to be saturated with emotion. As Robert and I left

his house to meet his daughters and their husbands and all five of his grandchildren, my thoughts turned again to Marti, wishing she were at my side to guide me through what lay ahead.

I'd been having fantasies, as Robert knew, that I could be another Marti and that his kids would come to love me as much as I'd loved her. But in a gentle way, he set me straight as we were driving over to Carrie's house.

"My dear, you'll never be their Marti, but let's hope you'll be something else good to them." The difference was, he pointed out, that Bonnie's kids had all adored her. "You didn't feel the same about your mother, so Marti was the mother you wished you'd had." But, he said, he thought his children would warm to me just because of who I was. "I can see you being close to them as a friend."

I knew he was right. " I can settle for "friend," I thought to myself.

Carrie lived on a tree-lined street in Westwood in a 1920s Spanish-style house. She came to the door to greet us with a beautiful warm smile. Kids were laughing and shrieking in the background. She took the present we'd brought for Jeremy and walked us into the living room, splashed with light and color.

My eye immediately went to the photo on the mantle of the fireplace: a radiant young Bonnie, who must have been a mother by then, dressed to teach a dance class. No doubt about it, she'd been lovely.

"We had the house cleaned for you," she said.

"I'm the last person you ever need to clean for! I am just happy to be here."

She seemed actually glad, I thought, to meet me and see her dad. I hoped that was so. But I suspected she felt as shy and awkward as I did.

She looked the way Robert had described her—a little like Reese Witherspoon, with her long blond hair tied into a knot above the nape of her neck. Her casual poise was like Jackie's, and probably her mother's. I was too dressed up; she wore jeans and a good-looking sweater with stylish flats.

She took me right off on a tour of the house, which was brimming with charm, and I felt the ice begin to break a little. In the master bedroom, all Robert's grandchildren were jumping around on the bed.

"Hey, will you say hello to Berto's friend Peggy and stop jumping for a minute."

They each shook my hand, looked me straight in the eye, and said hello. Carrie's boys, Jeremy, four, and Gabe, nine, were knockouts. And so were Jackie's kids. I met Ellie, the oldest one of the bunch, a friendly, pretty ten-year-old with long dark hair. Joey, nine, gave me a shy gentle smile. And that darling boy with the dimples, I thought, must be Sammy, whom I'd been told was three. He was an unstoppable jumper and the most impish of the five. They were curious about me for a second and very polite, but eager to get right back to jumping on the bed. I couldn't wait to get to know them.

After the tour of the house, Carrie disappeared into the kitchen to bring out the pizza she had ordered and a Caesar salad. She had told me she loved to read cookbooks but that cooking really wasn't her thing.

I wanted to offer to help her serve but was afraid she would think me too pushy. So, I joined Robert, who was chatting with his two sons-in-law. I sat there, flushed with gratitude.

Then the children trooped in, and everything felt much more relaxed by the time we all ate and the birthday boy blew out the candles on his cake and opened his presents with a dramatic ripping of paper. When Jeremy said with a little disappointment, "Every present I got is a book," I was very glad we'd also brought him a card with cash inside for sports shoes. "He's a great basketball and baseball player and his feet grow like crazy," Robert had told me.

What would Marti have done right now? I asked myself, still uncertain what role to play. She would have helped pick up the wrapping paper and followed Carrie into the kitchen. So, I did just that. "Your boys are darling," I said to Carrie as I helped her bring in the cake plates. After I snatched an extra swipe of frosting and popped it in my mouth, she did the same and we agreed with a good laugh that frosting was always the best part. That warm little moment made it easier to say, "Thank you for inviting us, Carrie. I know today isn't a simple one for you."

She gave me an answer as straight as the one I'd gotten from Jackie. "We are all happy to have you and Dad here, and you are right it is a hard day for everyone." I shot her a smile, but my eyes would have become teary if I'd stayed a moment longer.

I wandered back into the living room and made a point of sitting next to her husband Cary, who by chance has the same name as hers, just spelled differently. As he made room for me on the sofa, I complimented him on his boys and asked him about his work at Disney. I didn't get much more than a "fine." But then he surprised me by saying he loved Annie Lamott's writing and that Jackie had told him I knew her.   "Please tell her that her books were helpful to me when I became a father." I was glad we at least had that connection. I told Cary how much Robert enjoyed going to the boys' Little League games (although he hadn't been invited to them lately). I was hoping Cary would get the hint and issue an invitation to both of us, but he only did so indirectly. "You might get lucky when you come," he said, "Bob Dylan shows up from time to time to watch his grandson play."

Scott, Jackie's husband, came over and asked how I was doing. "I guess it's a pretty big day for all of us," I said. "I'm touched that everyone is so kind and friendly."

"Well of course, we are all happy that you're here," Scott said.

I had a little chat with Jackie about her kids and what she was reading. And then we got ready to leave. We hadn't stayed long, but long enough. As we got back in the car, I told Robert the party had gone better than I could have imagined. Bonnie was irreplaceable—I knew that as well as her daughters did. Carrie and Jackie were great young women; and they were all grown up, they didn't need a stepmother. They needed someone who would take good care of their father and be good to them and their kids.

Robert seemed deep in thought as we drove back to his house. He told me I had to understand that for his children our romance represented the loss of another parent, just months after the death of their mother. That day he'd been struck for the first time by the realization that when he moved to San Francisco, he'd be seeing much less of his daughters and his grandchildren even though we'd try to be around as much as possible. I knew that was going to be hard for him and that his children would need to have their time alone with their dad whenever we were in LA.

"You'll see, Peggy. Everything is going to work out," he told me "because we're all good people. Nobody thought you were a dog," he added with a grin, and leaned down to pet Cosmo.

Chapter Eighteen

MOTHER'S DAY HADN'T BEEN EASY, but it marked a turning point, a first step toward the slow mingling of our lives with Carrie's and Jackie's, and one day, Cass's.

Before school let out, we went to a couple of Little League games, rooting in the bleachers with the other parents and grandparents for Jeremy and Gabe. We never saw Bob Dylan, but we ate tropical fruit sprinkled with lime and chilies from a tiny cart in the park. Nobody knew how ecstatic I was to consider myself a quasi-grandmother. I loved watching those boys out there on the field batting and running their little hearts out, those boys who had come into my life by immaculate conception.

As summer rolled along, we felt increasingly comfortable taking the family out to dinner or meeting

at the Getty Museum. On one of our visits to the Getty, after we'd seen a few exhibits, I assembled everyone for a photograph. I took out my iPhone, aimed it, and asked a gray-haired passerby to take the picture. We smiled, all eleven of us as she fumbled over the proper button to press while we tried to hold still. Jackie suggested that next time I ask someone under 25 to shoot the picture. That provided us with our first full family laugh and our ongoing inside joke. Another small milestone.

Robert and I spent about half our summer at his house. He'd put it on the market in the worst month of the worst year in recent history for real estate sales. He didn't stage it because by now with so much removed to San Francisco, it was sufficiently spare.

In view of the dearth of prospective buyers, the agent asked Robert to drop the price again, and again.

We remained optimistic because we refused to let anything dampen our love, but silently we worried. Our anxiety was fueled by the accompanying decline of the stock market and the realization that large bills for Bonnie's care would keep arriving daily in the mail. It had been six years since Robert had worked and I'd written nothing for about half a year.

Besides the concern about introducing Robert's dogs to my cats, was the nagging question of how four dogs would fit into my small house. I was attached to Cosmo and Darlin' the bulldog. Those two I could handle. But Baby, the Frenchie, and Lily, the old, weak, petit vendeen basset griffon were another story. Baby would be too frisky for my cats, and I worried that the move would be too much for Lily.

One day while we were having lunch in the garden, Baby grabbed my new sunglasses, ate them, and spat them up—right on my foot. She'd been the one who'd grabbed my bra the first day I came to Robert's house. Sorry, but she was just not my favorite and apart from her, I was quickly becoming a serious dog lover.

We talked and talked about what to do. Rosa, the Fisher's loyal, longtime housekeeper, heard about our dilemma and offered to take Lily, as well as Baby. We could see them when we came to town to be with the kids, and we could pay for their care. She was sad about never seeing Cosmo and Darlin' again once we moved. With deep gratitude to her, we vowed to make it all happen.

Cosmo and Darlin' were always with us as we drove between our houses, curled up in the back of the Mini.

Cosmo would release a whole body shake that rattled the ID tags on his collar to let us know he smelled the familiar smoggy LA air on the freeways near Robert's house. He still considered it home. I hoped one day he'd do that as we approached the cool clear air in San Francisco.

The mingling of our animals hadn't been worth our worry. The animals ignored each other after the mandatory sniffing occurred every morning.

Now that I felt more at ease with Jackie and Carrie, I decided to prepare a big spare rib dinner for Robert's family. I spent the day making corn pudding, salads, and a large meringue, covered with whipped cream and fresh berries. I hoped the dinner would be appreciated, and I honestly think it was. One member of the family who shall remain nameless, quietly asked Robert if it was disturbing to him that I didn't clean everything up before sitting down for dinner. Unlike Bonnie, I left pots and pans in the sink.

Robert said that cooks have various habits in the kitchen and Peggy likes to join the table as soon as she finished cooking.

In my last cookbook, Simple Soirées, one of my steadfast dinner party precepts was to leave the dishes unwashed until everyone had gone home. I felt it was rude for the cook to be doing them while guests were still there. I was touched, however, when husbands Cary and Scott offered to clean up afterwards.

The next morning Scott called to say thank you for the great meal and to tell me how good it was to have the family kitchen used again. I'd always love him for that.

After all that was happening in Los Angeles, it was time for a big change of scenery. Summer wasn't summer to me unless I visited Mary and Bob Estrin at their ranch in New Mexico. I was dying to bring him to their ranch. It would be an entirely new experience for him since he knew New Mexico as he knew Paris, from the point of view of a tourist staying in fancy hotels.

"You'll love it there," I promised. "It's breathtaking to wake up in the high desert to masses of big extravagant cumulus clouds floating by."

We hiked in the rough desert terrain early in the mornings, hung around the old ranch house reading, doing jigsaw puzzles, and chatting during the heat of the day. After dinner, we collected branches and sagebrush and lit huge bonfires. One afternoon as I was waking up from a nap, I caught sight of a red flash streaking past the window. It was Robert galloping by on a horse. Mary must have talked him into riding, and he loved it, even if he walked bowlegged for a few days. While he'd told me he could ride, I was quite surprised by his horsemanship.

Other old friends gathered at the ranch as we had all been doing for the past thirty summers. I felt a certain pride to have brought Robert into the fold. No subject of interest was left unturned as we hung out and chatted. The Obama election was a hot topic and so were the summer Beijing Olympics. And we had all reached that age where we found some fascination in discussing our health. Robert was once again in total command of an endless array of topics--anything, that is, except the '60s and '70s. His memory was precise, his energy and positive nature were infectious. Separately, each of my friends took me aside to tell me how perfect he was for me.

I was just sorry that my childhood friend Ingrid, and her husband Harvey Kornspan were not there this visit. Same went for my dear friends the Kleins. It wasn't the same without them.

I don't think Robert had ever conversed so intimately with a group of friends, the women especially. We'd been close since the late sixties and by now, had few secrets. We were used to getting down to a pretty basic level, and I don't mean just talking about sex, but there was that too.

"As I told you, Bonnie and I didn't have single women friends," Robert mused one night as we were getting into bed. Your friends know so much about so many subjects. I am learning a lot, hearing you talk to one another. You keep blowing my mind, Peggy, to borrow a phrase."

CHAPTER NINETEEN

B y fall of 2008, about eight months into our romance, we'd settled into a relaxed morning routine in San Francisco. A normal day began around 6:00 a.m. when Darlin' would let out a gravelly chain of barks from the dogs' room downstairs. Robert would pull on his jeans and a sweater and take the two dogs across the street to the path above the park and alongside the old reservoir. The view of the bay, interrupted only by two expansive pine trees, would be his payoff for having to get up at the cold crack of dawn.

"Too many strange characters lurking about," he'd insist whenever I offered to walk the dogs.

I'd still be in bed when they came home. Darlin' and Cosmo would race up the stairs to get to me, squealing and wiggling until I got out of bed and lifted them up.

Lola and Lucie, the cats had staked out their spots right next to me. After a bit of rustling around, the dogs would always find a pillow or a body part to lie upon. I'd look out on the bay once again as Robert brought me my first cappuccino.

How did my life get so good so fast?

On early September mornings, the three masts of the Balclutha, a square-rigged historic ship docked in the water at the foot of our hill, were often hidden by fog. One day as we were reading the paper, Robert asked me about its history. I told him that the ship, originally British, had been used to carry Scotch whisky to San Francisco in exchange for grain. But then, I surprised myself by remembering that in 1959 the oddball comedian, Jonathan Winters climbed the masts and made a ruckus getting to the top. When the police were called, he ignored their pleas to descend. They finally grabbed him, threw him into a paddy wagon, and took him off to the psychiatric ward of SF General. I was very pleased when Robert said, "It's amazing you can remember all that." Lately, I'd wondered if my memory was getting shaky. My grandmother as well as my father had suffered from Alzheimer's and at my age, the fear was never far from my mind.

Robert had been having his own feelings of mortality. One morning he said to me, "I want to spoil you, so when I die, any potential suitor will appear worthless and you won't marry him."

"Yes, my love," I answered, "But if I wasn't that into marrying *you*, in the beginning, why do you think I would marry someone else? And what about you marrying some old nag after I die? I suppose you can, but you can't ever have sex."

Robert had segued into retirement when Bonnie got sick. But he had not totally adjusted to the concept, so he stayed plugged in with various consulting jobs. He'd never thought of himself as a businessman, even though he'd had considerable success. His real interests had always been leadership and putting people and companies together, and that was what he was pursuing now.

I wasn't really working those first months we were together, since some of the magazines I wrote for had either gone under, such as *Gourmet*, or had changed ownership, like *Saveur*.

As a result, we had plenty of time to explore San Francisco. We went to museums and downtown to Union Square. We went to the country and up the coast to visit friends and my brother and sister-in-law, Tony and Mary. We spent a lot of time walking the dogs. I was absolutely crazy about both of them and I wished I hadn't spent so much of my life without one.

Tony and Robert had taken to each other. Tony would call Robert to see if he wanted to have lunch on a day that he was coming to town. Robert would check and answer, "Well, the only thing I have on my calendar is bringing in the garbage cans."

He'd take me along on his shopping expeditions, picking up treasures for his grandchildren, birthday presents for our friends, and treats for me. I'd often told him he shopped like a Frenchman, because like a Parisian *flâneur*, he liked taking breaks at cafés and stopping to look into the windows, especially those of some of my own favorite small stores—Sue Fisher King and The Gardener. Since we didn't always agree on what we liked, our differences of opinion could lead to some spirited whispering in the stores.

In contrast, whenever we spent an evening at home, dinner was a two-way collaboration. I cooked the vegetables and made the salads; he grilled the meat or chicken or fish. Robert had grown to like most of my cooking, but I knew he always longed for Bonnie's double-baked potatoes and thicker, more marbled cuts of meat.

We never argued over money. Just his huge, over-the-top-wine glasses that he insisted on using for our friends that did drink wine.. Bonnie continued to drink wine after Robert stopped and they always poured wine from Robert's extensive cellar when they had parties. I went for less elaborate glasses. I found the big ones pretentious, but I didn't tell him that.

We also argued over my old boyfriends. Until the moment someone mentioned an old boyfriend, our life was heaven. Then hell would break loose. An unsuspecting friend would refer to a concert I'd gone to with some man I'd totally forgotten, and the questioning would begin. "Robbie," I'd plead, "we have it so good. Don't let some ghost ruin our precious time."

He thought I'd had scores of men, when in fact, I hadn't. Even a movie could set Robert off. Once when we were watching *Blowup*, he said he could imagine me in mod London, carefree and beautiful like Julie Christie, going to glamorous parties like the ones on the screen. Movies of women, wild and out of control, seemed to be running in his head. Truth be told, as rowdy as I'd been in my youth, I'd never gone to parties with men in white turtlenecks who drove red sports cars as in *Blowup*. It was all so crazy, so blown totally out of proportion.

On one of those difficult days when Robert couldn't stop questioning me about my lurid past, I suggested that we find a gym that would suit us both, hoping this distraction would calm him down. We checked out the Y in the Presidio and the Jewish Community Center on California Street. It was my misfortune that as we climbed the stairs to the gym at the JCC, we were confronted by a human-sized cardboard cut-out photograph of a man in boxing gloves sparring with a trainer. My heart sank as I recognized that figure—he was my last boyfriend. I hoped Robert wouldn't recognize him. No such luck— he'd seen him in snapshots. As we were leaving, he said, "Everywhere I go, I am struck with a vivid image of one of your boyfriends. Will this never end?"

I repeated over and over that I'd lived in this city all my life. By 63, I knew a lot of people. "This is your problem, Robert, not mine."

I asked Christopher for advice. To my surprise, she found it touching that Robert was jealous. Even she, a perfect human being, couldn't fully grasp how absurd

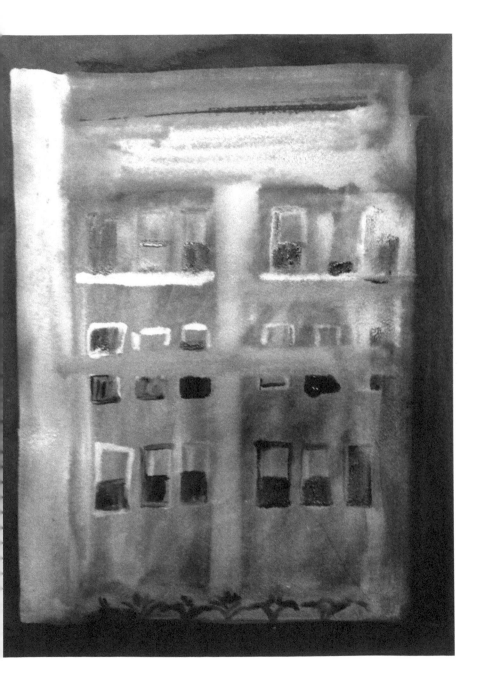

Robert's behavior was and how it troubled me. And my close friend Angie Thieriot, hands down, the most beautiful woman in San Francisco, and who was, like Christopher, as close to a perfect human being as they come, understood Robert's jealousy. That came as a surprise for how could a woman so serene from meditating since she was fifteen, ever feel a sense of jealousy? If she could, then it allowed for more compassion for Robert.

Still, I begged Robert to get some professional help for his obsession, pointing out that it was now the only obstacle to our romance, and suggested that he look around for a shrink. I knew better than to suggest one; Robert had to find a referral of his own. He'd had a lot of therapy, and he believed in it. He had first gone to a shrink when he and Bonnie argued about their different approaches to child-raising. When she got sick, he went back again because of depression. He was still seeing his L.A. therapist when I met him and spoke to one in St. Louis from time to time.

Friends of his recommended an old hippy Marin County psychologist, whom I'd heard about. When Robert came home from his first session, he told me that he'd been asked to role-play episodes from his childhood. This wasn't going to work, I thought, but I didn't say a word.

He went back for a couple more sessions, however, and he was apparently helped. He explained to me that he had grown to realize what had been happening. The fact that he was a competitive, but at times romantically insecure, alpha male was a major part of his problem. He'd rolled all of my men up into a single profile— one ideal man who was taller, smarter, richer, funnier, and better read than he. "I saw them as more erudite, tougher, cooler, and hung like a fucking bull moose, and I hated the sons of bitches."

I was cheered by what he seemed to have gathered from his short-lived therapy and wanted to believe the obsession had been lifted, but I still dreaded the possibility that an incidental remark could bring on another seizure, another couple of days of silence, another very cold shoulder.

In the meantime, we were continuing to take steps toward getting together permanently. Deciding we only needed one car, we sold Robert's. But he'd been a flatlander all his life so driving my standard shift Mini and parking on San Francisco's steep hills wasn't easy for him. We'd be in a parking garage and he'd get the gears mixed up and slam into a concrete pole. Accidents kept happening when he paralleled parked, too—so many, in fact, that we stopped filing insurance claims. The guys at Lombard Collision became our new best friends. Before we knew it, they were on Robert's speed dial. He called so often, the owner recognized his voice, "Hello Mr. Knickerbocker. Oh no, what is it this time?"

Robert had evidently decided he'd get better service around San Francisco if he referred to himself as Robert Knickerbocker. He used that name when he called the vet or made restaurant reservations. But to me, he said it with some residual resentment, "I really don't mind, but I don't think many of your friends actually know my last name. And by the way, have *you* learned it yet, Peggy?"

I had finally stopped calling him Robert Schneider. In fact, the real Robert Schneider came for a visit and the two of them got along swimmingly, discussing food and dogs. We had a good laugh over the way I'd confused their names.

Robert had a way of making irritating things seem funny. He was a lighthearted guy. Except when he wasn't. His jealousy would hibernate for a while, and then something would make him nuts again. One day a newspaper clipping from the 1970s with my picture in it fell out of a book he was reading. It had appeared in a local column called The Question Man. Each day The Question Man, who was actually a North Beach woman, would pose a question to passersby, and once I had been the one chosen to answer.

What is your weakness? My response had been, "Peonies, tequila, French movies, Samoan men, calamari, garlic, Ed Rusha, and Double Bubble gum." In the accompanying photograph, my long hair was tied back with a scarf, and I wore my favorite low-cut hippie dress that laced up to the breast. That photo was enough to make Robert start spewing a firestorm of questions. "What Samoan men? So, Ed Ruscha was another of your lovers? Did you always go around like that with your breasts practically showing?' He would not quit.

I told him I was going swimming and that when I returned, I would answer exactly three more of his questions. After that, I'd be done. If this continued, I warned him, we would have to go to the divorce judge before we even got married. I meant every word. I couldn't take the badgering one more day.

At the Dolphin Club, I lay on the beach in the sun for a few moments, sifting the sand through my fingers, as I gathered the courage to get in the cold water. I set a goal for my swim and made the plunge. Afterward, feeling invigorated and steadfast, I walked the three blocks to my house, opened the door, and said, "Okay, three questions only."

Once we got that over with, I told Robert I had something to tell him something I'd thought about while I was out swimming.

"You are the man I've been waiting for all my life. But I don't want to keep saying that. Either believe me or I will be the one moving on. I cannot handle your insanity."

"I hear you," said Robert.

"Robert," I continued, "I refuse to be called to account for any part of my life. Whatever I've experienced, I know I've always been a good and kind person—the person you tell me you love today. I've taken care of addiction, I've worked like a dog, and I'm over apologizing for myself, dammit." I spoke with a fury he'd not heard in my voice. "You are going to have to educate yourself about the time I lived in San Francisco. If you can't, this is absolutely not going to work." Completely exhausted, I sank into the sofa with Cosmo licking my wet red cheeks.

After my tears had dried, I told Robert that I'd been jealous, at times too, when my imagination had run wild.

I'd found that state of mind to be agonizing. But I'd come to understand that the best thing to do was to let the disturbance go.

Robert admitted that his periodic outbursts were fundamentally uncontrollable. They came out of the blue. An innocent remark about some incidental moment of my life triggered him. He felt very embarrassed by his flare-ups and was doing everything he could to get them under control before they burst forth. Often, he'd been successful.

"I never want to feel like a cuckold," he said plaintively. When he asked if I would do one thing to give him peace of mind—just tell him if we happened to be at the same party with someone I'd been with—I felt that wasn't too much for him to ask and said that I would.

Robert had never heard a jealous word from me about Bonnie. This was because Robert had made me feel from the beginning that he considered his life with her totally separate from his life with me.

His tantrums became less frequent as we moved on. When they did occur, I'd plead, "Let's not go there, Robert, please." Then I'd leave him alone for a while. He'd sulk quietly, watch a ball game and slowly be able let it go.

CHAPTER TWENTY

ENOUGH OF ALL OF THIS NONSENSE. We agreed not to spend one more minute on unfounded jealousy. "Let's take a trip to Paris before we do another thing," I suggested. Robert immediately grabbed at the idea and started looking up airline schedules. Soon we added a few days in New York as a stopover. Since he's a Taurus and I'm a Leo—not that either of us believes in astrology—we teased each other about the prospect of a bull and lioness taking a transatlantic trip together when just packing the car for a drive to L.A. posed problems.

Robert picked the hotel where we would stay in New York—the Elysée—because it was small, French, and romantic.

Years ago, a friend of mine, Laurel Gonsalves, with whom I'd stayed so many times in New York, that her

doormen knew my name, worked at Rolling Stone Magazine. She and her friends there used to call it the Easy Lay because apparently, it was the just the spot for trysts. I knew that for Robert it would be a far cry from the Four Seasons, where he usually stayed when he was in New York on business.

We spent a few hectic and satisfying days in the City, where we saw two plays and the Francis Bacon show at the Met. A nude self-portrait of Bacon's rear end caught my eye. I told Robert that the two men had something in common. They looked alike from that perspective. I think he liked that.

Robert met some of my old friends and I met some of his. They had little in common. One of my friends was dating the porn star, Jamie Gillis, at the time. It didn't matter, it was autumn in New York and we were in love.

We flew off to Paris. On the plane, Robert said he'd had a great time being in the city with me but pointed out that I definitely had my own way of being there. As a traveler, he was used to being more laid back while I was used to tearing around on foot until I dropped dead and had to go home for a nap. "I'm not that way," he said, "but I love that you are."

Once in Paris, he asked me to lead the way. He had been there a number of times himself, but Paris is my second city. I'd already arranged for us to stay in a friend's pied-a-terre, which had been my base during the years before I bought my own place. Robert had never set foot in a Parisian apartment. He didn't understand the French lighting system in the building's communal spaces. "This is not what I expected," Robert told me after he dropped our bags to look around the apartment. I immediately took him out to the balcony and steered his gaze to the street below, to the Edgar Quinet open-air market that was in full swing. I grabbed his hand and said, "Let's go down before unpacking and buy flowers and cheese and fruit. You never got to do this when you stayed at George V, did you?" By the time we'd shopped and then gone out for our first neighborhood dinner, he was mad about our cozy bohemian apartment.

I was so eager to give Robert experiences he'd never had, that the pace in Paris was hectic, too. We ate at non-touristy places, saw my French and expatriate friends, and visited several of my favorite small, esoteric museums, including the eccentric Deyrolles, a curiosity and taxidermy store and museum all in one.

After our first day or so, I took him by my old apartment on Rue Madame, a block away from the Luxembourg Gardens in the 6th *arrondissement*. As we stood in the courtyard looking up at the building where I'd lived on and off for five years, we both wished I hadn't sold it just before meeting him.

We drove to Chateau Courances with friends from California who spent a lot of time in Paris. Our mutual friends had the gardener's cottage on the grounds of the grand old chateau about thirty miles south of Paris, on the western edge of the Forest of Fontainebleau. Our hosts were among my closest friends in Paris—Richard Overstreet, the American expatriate artist who was married to French filmmaker, Agnès Montenay.

Robert's jaw hung wide open as they led us over moats, through forests, along a great expanse of gardens, by pools and ponds and down an alluring allée of trees. At night after dinner, the five of us sat in front of a fire, talking, and laughing, and looking at books. So much for Robert's not wanting to stay with friends.

For our last night in Paris, we'd arranged to take Randal Breski out for his birthday dinner. He'd helped me with the design of my house in San Francisco. After returning from the country late, we rushed to meet him at a restaurant on the Île Saint-Louis. It was raining, the streets were wet and slick, and Robert was wearing his beautiful, new, slippery shoes. He missed a curb and fell hard on the pavement with a loud slap on his back and hip. I was horrified to see him writhing in pain. As I helped him up, I felt like such a jerk for hurrying him along when we couldn't find a cab. But the next day, after a few last-minute visits to cheese shops and men's stores, he seemed absolutely fine. Mission accomplished, we both agreed. We had proved we could travel quite well together, and we had not had one fight about my past.

Chapter Twenty One

WE WERE THRILLED WHEN WE RETURNED to San Francisco to a note from Jackie inviting us for Thanksgiving in Los Angeles.

For the Fishers, Thanksgiving had always been a very big deal. Bonnie's lavish meals were a family legend. The repertoire had included recipes passed on to her by her family's beloved cook, Edell, who had also helped raise the three children before the move from St. Louis to New York and on to Los Angeles. Jackie, an excellent cook, was determined to carry on her mother's traditions.

Thanksgiving had been my favorite holiday, as well. My mother would let me make the cornbread stuffing with lots of chopped herbs, celery, and the bacon fat she'd been saving in a Folger's coffee can. I also made the hard sauce to go with the persimmon pudding and prepared little onion puffs for hors d'oeuvres. My mother put orange zest and brown sugar into her sweet potatoes along with a good deal of dark rum. She'd sneak a few nips of rum as she was cooking. She was a snob and always mentioned her prejudice against the use of marshmallows on top of sweet potatoes. I loved those old recipes and had fond memories of the dozens of Thanksgivings when I'd cooked for family and friends over the years. The guests had changed but my menu rarely veered from my mother's.

Now that I was about to become a member of a new family, I found that my lingering sentimental feelings about my family recipes were not as strong as they once had been. Honestly, I was getting a little tired of my usual Thanksgiving and was looking forward to someone else's cooking, a fresh take on the meal, and some youthful energy to do the heavy lifting.

As Robert was getting used to my cooking, he'd bring up the ways Bonnie made things for him. "Why do you make these chocolate chip cookies so small and crisp?" he'd ask. "Have you ever thought about making them softer and bigger?"

"Oh I bet Bonnie made them like that," I'd respond.

To which he'd reply, "Oh yes, I can taste them now."

"Good, my love, hold that memory, because I don't make them like that."

Although we could joke around, Robert warned me that his daughters took their mother's cooking very much to heart. "They think she was the best cook in the world. I am sure it is one of the things they miss most about her."

I promised him that I would never try to insinuate my Northern California style of cooking within the family. "I get what a sensitive subject it is," I told Robert. "I was protective of Nancy Knickerbocker's way of doing things, even though I didn't like her as much as Marti." Luckily for me, Marti had little interest in cooking. Her only specialty was a Roquefort hors d'oeuvre made with puff pastry. She left Thanksgiving to Tony and me.

It was for cooks like Bonnie that I wrote my books and articles—good cooks, interested cooks," I told Robert. "Don't you remember how her baking drawer took my breath away, how I could sense her in your kitchen when I saw her carefully arranged equipment?"

"Jackie will carry the torch, Robert told me, "Until the next generation takes over."

I assured him that I'd do whatever Jackie wanted me

to, or I'd stay entirely out of the way. Robert and I were the elders now, I realized.

A few days before we left for LA, I called Jackie to see what we could contribute. I told her I was looking forward to her mother's recipes and asked what I could do. She asked me to make a pear upside-down cake. I told her I'd be delighted and that we would also take care of getting the turkey. Robert would supply the wine.

The day before Thanksgiving, Jackie and I had fun setting the table and cooking together. It was brand new for me not to be in charge, but I felt I was handling it well, and so was she. I admit I was relieved, happy to be by her side. I didn't make a single suggestion.

Earlier that morning, Robert and I took two of his grandsons, Gabe and Jeremy, to the farmers' market in Santa Monica to buy some additional produce. The boys had never been there, but they were great sports about it and curious about the exotic fruits we pointed out. They even learned the names of two types of persimmons—Fuyu and Hachiya.

After the market, it was time to have some fun, so we went down to the beach. We all took our shoes off, even Robert who doesn't like to, because he's not a California boy. We hid them behind a lifeguard station, a daring act for three males very much attached to their shoes. We played tag, all of us running as fast as we could, until we flopped down on the sand. The beach made us feel free. We lost ourselves for those few moments, shrieking and laughing, as we tried to escape the tags that would make us "it."

I had never dreamed I would have the chance to see myself as a grandmother. But look at me now, I thought to myself—lying exhausted and laughing in the sand with Robert and these two adorable boys.

When we returned to Jackie's with the pears for the cake, Joey, her middle son, wanted to help me bake. He was the kid in the family most interested in cooking. He and I assembled our ingredients. We lined the bottom of a pan with butter and brown sugar and a pinwheel of sliced pears. We had so much fun—just Joey and me. Both of us had a sweet tooth and we licked our fingers as we cooked. We poured on the batter and slipped the cake into the oven. We waited as it baked. It emitted a sweet buttery smell.

When it came out of the oven and cooled, we conferred, deciding it was time for the flip. "We have to get the bottom to become the top," I explained. "That's why it's called an upside-down cake." We loosened the removable side of the pan, put a plate on top of the cake, and got another plate ready for the flip back over. We held our breath. "Okay—let's go, and we made the flip. But it wasn't a flip; it was a flop. It went right on the floor.

We were both on the verge of tears. But you know what Julia Child would have done, and we did the same. We got a clean plate, took a spatula to scrape the splattered cake off the freshly mopped floor, and pieced it back together. We looked at each other, high-fived, and shared the first moment of a long-lasting love.

We realized we'd more or less succeeded when Joey's father came in and licked the spatula we'd used. "Is that ever good." Joey and I glanced at each other as if to say, our secret is safe.

Thanksgiving turned out to be sensational. Everyone was relaxed and hungry. There were masses of yellow roses on the long table with Jackie's collection of Beatrix Potter figurines that she put out for the kids. Bonnie's recipes were delicious. The sweet potatoes were made with marshmallows browned on top. I devoured at least two helpings—and to think I'd been disparaging of the marshmallows just like my mother.

The next day Robert and I stopped by with the dogs to say goodbye and to thank Jackie for doing a great job and for keeping the family tradition together. Robert told her how proud her mother would have been, how proud he was of her. We were all feeling the love. The holiday had presented us with a confirmation that we were moving ahead as a family.

Among leftovers to take back with us to San Francisco, Jackie gave us a plate of her dark crackly brownies. I don't even like brownies, but these were like fudge. To stop myself from eating them all, I had to move them to the very back of the car.

CHAPTER TWENTY TWO

D URING OUR DRIVE HOME, Robert said he was feeling a sharp pain in his right hip. Maybe he had pulled something while we were playing with Gabe and Jeremy, or perhaps it was from his fall on the slick Parisian street. It was bad.

I went with him later that week to see an orthopedic doctor. Dr. Vail took one look at Robert's x-rays and said, "You need a hip replacement. No point in living with the pain; it will just get worse."

We both felt stunned. We hadn't even lived together a year and now Robert was going in for a major operation and we were listening to the nurse tell us what equipment we'd need once he got home from the hospital.

He came to pick me up from an appointment with the rear end of the Mini fully loaded. A borrowed beige porta-potty was stuffed into the car along with a metal walker with cut-in-half-green tennis balls stuck onto the ends of the legs.

"Is this what I signed up for—a man with a porta-potty and a walker?" I teased him. "I can see why marriage vows include, "in sickness and in health." I wondered—if he'd hooked up with a twenty-five-year-old, where would she be now?

I made light of his operation, but my God. This was serious. I'd seen my father through two hip replacements. I wondered what sort of a patient Robert would be, how he'd heal.

Jackie came to stay for the operation, to be there for her dad. I was happy to have her company. We got crab salads from Swan to eat while the procedure took place.

The operation reminded me of one my father had in 1969. He had been among the first to have a new type of hip replacement. My family waited for news of the operation while watching Tiny Tim's marriage to Miss Vickie on the Tonight Show.

By the time he was out of the hospital, Robert wanted to get well fast. He was a great patient. He did as he was told, and I loved taking care of him. His positive attitude made it easy.

I coaxed him off the sofa a few times a day to take little walks along the passageway behind our house. By the time he got an encouraging word from the doctor, after his first post-op appointment, he suggested we go out for lunch.

He was proud that he'd been so easy to take care of, and I was glad that my patience had grown to the point that I never lost it. We appeared to be handling the first indication of the aging process quite well together.

Chapter Twenty Three

WE HAD DECIDED TO GET MARRIED on Valentine's Day, the anniversary of our first date. So, we started thinking about arrangements for our wedding as soon as Robert began to recover.

For his first wedding in 1963, Robert had not been involved in any of the planning; he'd been happy to leave everything to Bonnie and her mother. For my first wedding, I'd had nothing but nonnegotiable ideas. It had to be on a beach, and I'd insisted on a cheesecake wedding cake, a cake that my mother and father were going to cut, because I didn't like the custom of the bride and groom stuffing cake into each other's mouths. In fact, my 1968 wedding was all about the food, the clothes, the locale, the fun of planning, announcements in the paper, the little honeymoon, and the presents. Oh, and of course I

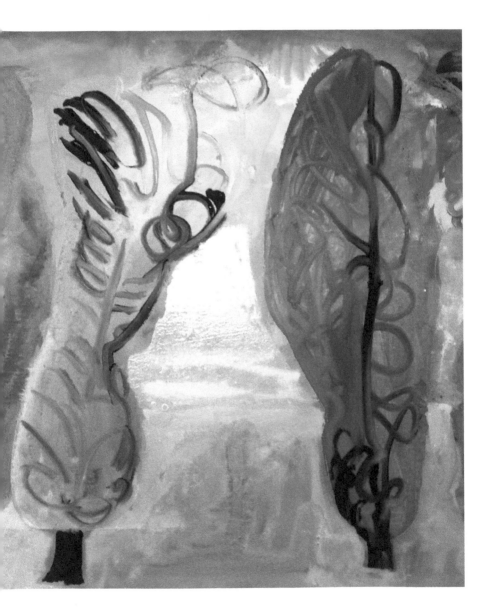

loved Jay Hanan, but today, I think we'd both agree, it was as if we were playing at getting married. We were only twenty-two. What did we know? My poor mother had to deal with her darling daughter who thought she knew everything there was to know about weddings. Marriage, not so much.

As for this upcoming wedding, neither Robert nor I knew where to start. But this time, the marriage was the object; the wedding was merely the formality. We were making a pact to grow old together. The vows would have an entirely new meaning this time around. "In sickness and in health; until death do us part." Those phrases were far more compelling now than they were in our twenties, when we thought we were immortal.

Our late-blooming love would not require us to raise a family, start careers, or put kids through college. It would be a more selfish partnership. We were marrying to love and support one another, to live the years we had together to the fullest, to relish our families and friends. For me, reality had set in even before Robert's operation. We had been out walking the dogs, crunching through dry autumn leaves, making a lot of noise, when for the first time I'd quietly confronted the question of how many autumns we would have left together. Ten, fifteen, if we were lucky, twenty?

Should our wedding be minuscule with just our two immediate families, or should we have a big celebration? We made a list of friends just to see how many we'd invite if we wanted a splashy affair. Quickly it came to 250 to 300 people.

I turned to my young friend Cristina Salas-Porras, who'd recently begun working as creative director at a small, luxe, ultra-contemporary hotel in the Napa Valley called Bardessono. With a mind to solving our problem, she suggested we marry there. Management assumed our wedding would be a big lively social event and draw attention to the hotel. They made a generous offer.

We drove to Napa for a tour. At first, it seemed that Bardessono would be an ideal setting—the hotel was both posh and green, built with salvaged cypress and redwood, and edged with massive Japanese rock arrangements. Neither Robert nor I had thought beyond the ceremony, but once we got started with Cristina and her colleagues, the conversation veered off to how the weekend would proceed. The weekend?

Of course, we'd want a Friday dinner to greet our

guests coming from across the country and beyond, such as Robert's brother, Richard, and sister-in-law Mary from St. Louis. And then there'd be the various hotel rooms we'd want to secure for them. Of course. Ching, ching, ching went the cash register in my brain. Robert's house still hadn't sold. Of course, we would offer our guests a Saturday breakfast and make arrangements for outings during the day. Then there would be the ceremony, followed by the reception and Sunday breakfast. It was almost as if the wedding was an afterthought. We discussed music, wine, food, decorations, flowers, and transportation. It wasn't that we didn't feel generous towards our guests and family, but what about us?

I started frowning without meaning to when Cristina described the luxurious spa features I could use to be fresh for the ceremony. A very small family gathering was gaining appeal by the minute. Robert and I thanked her and the others for the tour and said we'd discuss the plans over lunch. We walked across the street to my fiancé's favorite wine country spot, Bouchon, where we sat outside with the dogs. The pale December sun wasn't terribly enthusiastic. And neither, we found, were we.

We ordered frisée salads with lardons and poached

eggs. Robert had his usual Midwestern iced tea, and as for me, I wanted a martini something bad. I settled for water. Our salads came. The dogs cocked their heads and looked at me as if to say, What's wrong, Peggy?

Robert said, "You are uncharacteristically quiet. What's up? Why are you not touching your salad?"

Getting married at the hotel had been a delightful idea as we drove from the city and past Sonoma, into Napa and through acres of vineyards. The hotel was out of this world, and it would be absolutely perfect for a first wedding. But it would be an over the top production for our second, and a big extravagant wedding wouldn't be fair to Robert's children. I hadn't met Robert's son Cass and his wife Mariana. If they came, we couldn't even get to know each other. I began to feel quite ill. The hotel people had been so helpful and kind to us, but I knew we were biting off more than we wanted to chew.

Robert ate my salad and we were quiet for a couple of minutes. I called old friend Annie Lamott to see if she'd perform our ceremony, but she was on a book tour. Then in unison, we thought of our favorite judge, Chuck Breyer. He and I had grown up in the City at about the same time; I knew his wife, Sydney. "Let's ask Chuck to marry us on Valentine's Day," I suggested.

I was still feeling a bit weepy. Cosmo begged to get up on my lap to soothe me, and Darlin' licked my legs.

"Let's keep it simple," I finally said. "Just have Tony and Mary and any of your kids who want to come. We can have a delicious dinner at Chez Panisse and be done with it," I added feebly, as the espressos came.

Robert said that anything I wanted was fine with him.

I could tell he felt relieved. It had been fun to plan big for a while, but we felt much better now. I called Cristina to thank her. She understood our decision completely. The next call I made was to Chuck. Robert and he had become friendly over coffees at the farmers' market on Saturday mornings. He happened to be free on Valentine's Day and loved the idea that we wanted the dogs at our ceremony. He said he'd make all the arrangements.

When we got home from Napa, I asked Robert if I could see his wedding ring. The one he'd bought to replace his gold one. It would better match his belt buckles, not all of his 126 of them, just the ones that were silver. "Whatever," I said. "My mind is blown by your attention to detail that nobody else notices." It was a wedding ring he'd bought for himself while Bonnie was sick and he hadn't had it engraved. I pocketed it for an idea I had.

I asked the jeweler to engrave this inscription: RCF-BCF 1963 *** RCF-PK 2009. It had Robert's and Bonnie's initials and the year of their wedding, and his and mine and the upcoming year of our wedding. I kept it a surprise.

I've never been a diamond girl, or even particularly interested in jewelry, except for things I find unusual or over-the-top or fun to wear. I'd lost my mother's emerald and diamond engagement ring while making a huge mound of steak tartar for a party we were catering ages ago.

But a few days later, when we went to the fancy Union Square jewelry stores to pick out two rings for me, I got dressed up, as I'd done since the '50s whenever I went downtown. I no longer wore gloves, of course, or Mary Jane's with white socks. Instead, I wore my grey flannel coat with a high collar, an orange wool dress, and my new fancy leopard heels that Robert bought me to apologize for one of his crazy jealous fits.

We found a simple, handsome gold band with a nickel-sized yellow semi-precious stone as an engagement ring. It was from Shreve & Co., the store I'd gone to since I was a girl to get charms or St. Christopher medals for my friends' birthday presents. It was just the thing. Then we went to Cartier to get a very simple infinity ring for me in three colors of gold, just like Robert's colors. We had it fitted and engraved and didn't give it another thought until the wedding day. I went immediately to have a manicure so I could show my new ring to its best advantage. And did I flash it! I was beginning to believe I was getting married.

Our wedding was shaping up. It was a very big deal, but it was to be simple and with five or six guests only.

I told Robert, "I used to drive home from dinners in Marin across the Golden Gate Bridge before I met you. I'd think, isn't one of those sparkly lights home to a man who'd be perfect for me. Out of all of the men in San Francisco, there's got to be just one."

"My light," Robert said, "was shining in a gated community in LA, waiting for you."

I forget exactly how word about our wedding got around, but it was after Robert told his children and asked them to come, and after I told my family and friends.

Some of our friends offered to have parties. That pleased us no end. Our first one was given in L.A.

by Mary and Bob Estrin, whom we'd visited in New Mexico. During the afternoon, when we went over to help, we took a little siesta in a hammock by the pool. Darlin' snooped around the garden, Cosmo slept on my chest. Just as we dozed off we heard a terrible commotion. Darlin' had never seen a swimming pool. She saw a beach ball floating and saw no reason not to walk across the water to get it. Bulldogs do not swim. She sank instantly. Robert, bleary-eyed from napping, rolled off the hammock to see what happened. He raced to the edge of the pool and pulled her out by her collar. She sputtered and coughed and shook like mad. If he'd waited a minute longer, she'd have been a goner.

At the party that night, my friends and Robert's didn't really mingle, but no one seemed to care, and I wouldn't have known anyway. I was floating above the crowd, having a ball all on my own. When I explained to Robert where I go in situations such as these, he said, "You have me now, Peggy. I am here to ground you."

Shortly before our wedding, Robert and I went to a party in St. Louis, a city I'd never been to. I took photographs of him in front of each of the houses he'd lived in and was glad to put faces to the many people

Robert had told me about. I'd never been to St. Louis.

Robert introduced me to Bonnie's close friends. They went out of their way to be kind and inclusive. I'm sure some were curious to see me; the woman Robert had gone so crazy over when he'd had such a good long marriage with Bonnie. I did what Marti did when she met friends of my late mother's. She'd mention her predecessor's name. I did the same. Everyone in St. Louis missed Bonnie terribly. I found that it broke the ice to ask people to tell me what Bonnie was like.

Everyone was so damn nice in St. Louis. Parties were given for us in three clubs. I hadn't been in a country club since the Carter Administration. I got to try a couple of St Louis delicacies—toasted ravioli and Gooey Butter Cake and became an ardent fan of both.

Our date was set for Friday, February 13th. We weren't superstitious. Valentine's Day was out, since it fell on a Saturday when the Judge's chambers in the Federal Building would be closed. Robert asked my brother Tony to be best man, and I asked my sister-in-law Mary to stand up for me. Their job was to bring me a bouquet of white peonies and a sprig of daphne for Robert's buttonhole. They would also pick up a white cake with white frosting from our favorite bakery, Della Fattoria, in Petaluma on their way down to the city.

We waited to hear from Robert's children. Who would come? Whatever happened would be fine, Robert and I agreed. Carrie was still not exactly pleased with how her father had handled himself. He regretted his plea to her to throw confetti on our parade.

I am sure it hurt him when she told us she'd decided not to come. She wrote me a letter explaining why. She said it had nothing to do with me, but it rankled her that he was so insistent that she celebrate his newfound love along with him. She was still mourning after a year. I totally respected her decision. But Jackie would fly up from Los Angeles for the wedding and the celebration dinner at Chez Panisse.

We were terribly pleased when Cass and Mariana, Robert's son and daughter-in-law, agreed to come from Florida. We made reservations at a hotel near us and couldn't wait to spend time with them over the weekend. Their presence and Jackie's meant everything to Robert.

Christopher and Jim Hirsheimer flew out from Pennsylvania. Christopher, my dear, dear friend, and favorite photographer, offered to take pictures. She could have given us no better present. Our neighbor was away, so she let them stay next door. We rushed back and forth between the houses with the glee of twenty-year-olds.

Life was grand the day before our wedding. When Christopher and Jim arrived, we went to have our usual crab lunch at Swan. It was our habit to go whenever they came. We returned home and settled in, with not a thing in the world to do but relax and be grateful and make spareribs for dinner. Darlin' and Cosmo knew something was up. We bathed them so their coats were smooth and silky. They were going to be wearing white silk ribbons around their necks as they stood beside us before the judge.

Then all hell broke loose.

Susan Andrews called.

"Hey Peggy, you were my best woman when I got married, what's with not being invited to YOUR wedding? I'm sorry, I know where it is, and I'm coming," she said. "You can't get married without me. And what about your oldest friends?"

"Yikes, Susan, we were going to keep it very small, just

family. We will celebrate at parties in the spring."

"Peggy, you mean so much to me, and so does Robert. I flew to LA to meet him. I am coming."

"Okay, then. I can't refuse you," I said, only slightly chagrined. "We are having lunch afterwards at Hayes Street Grill. I'll call Patty and ask her for another place at the table."

"Oh God, there goes our peace," I lamented to Robert. "If Susan's coming, I want to invite Cal and Flicka. I've known them longer than Susan, than anyone." So, I called them, explaining why the invitation was so late, and asked them to join us at the judges' chambers and for lunch.

"I don't want anyone to feel left out," I said to Christopher, "but making all new plans less than twenty-four hours before our wedding isn't exactly how I saw this day,"

I got on the phone and called more people, some couldn't come at the last minute, some I forgot. Robert wanted to invite his dearest St Louis friends, not to mention his brother Richard, and his wife, Mary. I reached Patty Unterman at Hayes Street Grill to let her know the realistic number for lunch after the wedding. She assured me that she'd take care of everything.

We already had a small dinner celebration scheduled

at Chez Panisse for family. We'd reserved the little porch upstairs where we could barely fit and there was no room for add-ons. Alice Waters and I had worked out a most exquisite menu:

Buckwheat Blini and Steelhead Caviar

Grilled Anchoiade Toasts with Fennel,
Cardoon and Tardivo Salad

Wood-Oven-Roasted Quail
with Stinging Nettles and Green Garlic

Garden Lettuces à la Panisse

Blood-orange Pavlova

We'd added to our schedule a dinner at Zuni on Saturday for the people who'd had a hand in introducing us or counseling us. I worked out the menu with Gilbert Pilgrim, Zuni's co-owner, the man I'd traveled with in China. It included every one of my favorite dishes:

Piccolo Fritto di Cuore Misti

Bagna Cauda con Tartuffi Neri

Arista e Sformatto di Ortiche

Meringuatta Matrimonia—
a layered meringue wedding cake.

Christopher took me to get my hair blown the morning of the wedding. Barbara Mendelsohn met us at the beauty salon with more pearl necklaces for my wedding outfit. I'd decided on a Chanel look, even though nothing I'd chosen was actually Chanel. I would wear a crisp, high-collared white blouse under a fitted black ¾-length light wool coat, over a pair of flared black trousers—and as many pearl necklaces as I could find. I loved my outrageously pearly bling. Even my hair had turned out well. Surprisingly, I was not at all fluttery, unlike the hour before my first wedding when my mother had forced a Valium on me. In fact, I'd been overtaken by a surge of utter well-being.

I'd never thought it would happen, but I'd found the absolute perfect man and I was marrying him. I missed my parents and Marti and her last husband Jack Cowden much more than I expected, and wished they could have met Robert.

As I was dressing, Mary and Tony arrived with the flowers and cake, and Jackie was right behind, in a taxi. We had to call a car to take us to the Federal Building. It had started raining and we would have gotten wet. The dogs couldn't go with us because they didn't have a place to go while we had lunch.

On the way to our wedding, we picked Cass and Mariana up at their hotel. I looked at myself in the mirror, quite pleased with what I'd pulled off. It was very much over the top, with about eight necklaces and big Jackie O dark glasses since the sky was bright in spite of the rain. I thought, poor Cass, he'll think his dad is marrying a superficial woman who lavishes herself with way too much of everything.

When Cass and Mariana got into the car, it was awkward, but we were all together and off we went.

Guests were passing through the metal detector at the Federal Building by the time we arrived. I begged the guard not to make me take off all of my precariously fastened necklaces. He relented.

A few moments later, we were in the chambers, greeting everyone, but really, I had no idea who was there and who I'd forgotten. I took Robert's hand and said, "I'll be so happy when this is all over and we are back in bed with all the animals."

I looked around the room at some of my life-long friends who had always been enough and whose love had helped me create a rich, full, hilarious life and find peace in being single. They were now cheering me on into a life in which my beloved Robert had become the center, a perfect fit.

I finally got it right.

Afterwords
love later on

SINCE OUR WEDDING on February 13, 2009, Robert and I have walked most mornings at Crissy Field, an old Army helicopter base along the beach leading to the Golden Gate Bridge. The waves crash, the off-leash dogs run and play, and we see friends who, like us, are mesmerized by the rolling seascape.

On a windy Sunday morning, about six years ago, Robert lagged behind the dogs and me on the trail. We reached a bench at the little Warming Hut and he slumped. Cosmo and Darling tilted their heads, questioning our divergence. "I'm very dizzy," he said. "I'm not sure I can make it back."

That was in 2015, seven years into our marriage. Robert's grandchildren were happily matriculating, his children and he were peaceful and close after his transition away from them in Los Angeles to San Francisco.

We established our own traditions. Our life was splashed with art, politics, music, good food, and great friends. We were selfish with our time. We rarely did anything we didn't want to.

Robert made it slowly back to the car, that windy morning. For months afterwards, we tried to find a diagnosis. We lived at Kaiser Permanente visiting various departments, specialists in neurology, getting MRIs, and blood tests. We got second opinions. Everyone, including friends, had a theory—no one could figure out what Robert Fisher had, except that it was a degenerative disease of the nervous system.

First, it was one cane, then two. Robert exchanged his passion for buying shoes to collecting canes. When he'd amassed about twenty, he needed a walker. Not just any walker, a special Scandinavian brand. If he ventured into a store or restaurant thinking he didn't need his Volaris Rollator, his gait often mimicked that of a drunk.

About this time, our dogs died, first the bulldog and then the 15-year-old dachshund. I broke down. Somehow, I knew we'd handle Robert's illness. The sorrow over the dogs—we weren't so sure. We collected their ashes and put them in boxes on our Day of the Dead altar. We were inconsolable.

Then a baby bulldog appeared in our lives after weeks of research. She called herself Lovie. Lola and Lucie, our ragdoll cats, accepted her, once hierarchy was established. We gave up all other entertainment to watch the three of them play. She opened our hearts and gave us a built-in excuse to leave dinners early.

Today, in early 2021, we are no closer to a diagnosis than four years ago, other than it being a nonspecific, progressive neurological disease. Robert's life has grown wobblier. We keep walking.

Our romance is thriving. The house is filled with flowers, we keep the candles lit every night at dinner, and always go to sleep with a kiss. We take our time, one day at a time, and remain positive.

Some days, our big decision is what to have for lunch. I'm still writing, Robert is riveted by politics, reading incessantly and watching lots of TV news and sports.

He stays connected to his children and friends on his smartphone. We take utter delight in our five-year-old granddaughter and two great-nieces, and keep in touch with our older grandchildren. Otherwise, we remain involved with our families and friends, and leave lots of time to ourselves.

We count ourselves lucky because we took some great trips before it became too much for Robert. Now, with Robert's encouragement, I travel with my friends. We no longer hike or swim together. And, we can't visit Robert's children as we used to. Still, I wouldn't trade a day with Robert in his condition for anything. He loves being in our house and is curious to hear the news I bring home. I'm amazed when I hear women say they don't want to be a nurse or a purse. Not that I am either, but they haven't met Robert.

I'm convinced Robert came into my life at the ideal moment. I'd worked hard at my rough edges and was in a position to choose a man who was perfect for me. A man who never made me guess, but rather made me feel confident and adored. On every level and because of each other, we are closer to the people we've always wanted to be.

ACKNOWLEDGEMENTS

Huge thanks to my beloved friend, the artist Karen Barbour, illustrator extraordinaire for taking on our story with humor and tenderness. Her illustrations capture the mood and emotion of my story.

I'm grateful to Christopher Hirsheimer, my remarkable friend, who has taken to my writing and encouraged me since the beginning. She believed in our love and brought it to light on the page with an eye and delicacy that only she could convey. She rescued this work by designing this beautiful book.

Thanks to Margo True who was my first editor for this as well as my earlier stories at *Saveur* magazine. She laughed at our pratfalls and kept me on track.

I'm grateful to Joyce Johnson who taught me enough while editing my manuscript that I felt I earned an honorary masters in writing—and along the way, we became friends.

I thank agent Charlotte Sheedy for great suggestions and patience.

I acknowledge Kimberley Cameron for her creative attempts with my work and for sharing a love of Paris.

Sue Conley has nurtured my writing for many years. I am grateful for all those mornings when we read what we'd written to one another. I thank her for encouragement and love and for teaching me all about cheese. Our biggest celebration, out of the many she and Nan Haynes have shared, will be when this book sees the light of day.

Forever grateful to David Sheff for being the first to read the manuscript and for calling me in tears when he finished. He supported me since I bought my first computer. And he has been the impetus for the most affectionate, rowdy dinner of the year.

Armistead Maupin makes storytelling look easy. We have kept one long laugh going since I met him in North Carolina in 1966.

Anne Lamott has been a treasured friend and writing adviser for the sober lifetime we have shared for decades. A few years ago, she asked me if I was going to turn seventy-five without telling my best story yet. I am now seventy-five and have written that story.

Great thanks to Steven Barclay for making every angle of my life sharper and more French. He helped this book, and me, all along the way.

Liz Morten was an early treasure of my new life with Robert. We clicked because our love of writing. She brought me into a critique group that includes Gillian Foster, Lori Stewart, and Maggie Hardy who listened to the final drafts of *Love Later On*. And thanks to Gabi Coatsworth, who joined us subsequently from Connecticut, for casting her eyes on the finished manuscript for a final copy edit.

My beloved brother Tony Knickerbocker was, I think, aghast, when he read a first draft airing a bit too much family laundry and probably too much of my own. It was at this point that I realized my many years in twelve-step programs opened the doors to being unambiguous. My love and thanks to my darling nieces and nephew, their children and mates.

My sister-in-law Mary Lawler will, I suspect, be happy with how the family storieshave emerged. I am delighted to have a sister, a hiking partner, and someone who is always willing to share her infinite knowledge about family and our animals.

My deep thanks to Robert's adult children for reading early drafts and for putting up with their father's rash decision to move to San Francisco so abruptly. Carrie Fisher Okmin, Jackie Fisher Frager and Cass Fisher and their spouses, Cary Okmin, Scott Frager and Mariana

Fisher have accepted me unequivocally, along with their precious children.

My thanks to Richard and Mary Fisher, my brother and sister-in-law, for welcoming me into the family and supplying me with Fisher lore.

Cal Ferris started this story for me by introducing me to Robert through our mutual friend Steve Grand Jean and his wife at the time, Nan. When I thought it was over, she assured me it had just begun. She's been that kind of a sister since we were seven.

I am forever intertwined in my friendship with Flicka McGurrin since second grade. She has come to be a part of my new family as I've been a part of hers for decades. We've travelled the world, been business partners, swum in bodies of water we never dreamed of. I am godmother to Meighan, McGurrin and Lei, her cherished children.

I was Angie Thieriot's first friend when she moved to San Francisco in 1972. I've adored our friendship ever since. A writer, artist, and amazing cook, she's read more books than anyone I know. When she was gently critical of an early draft, I took note and made vital changes that improved not only the work, but myself as well.

Susan Andrews figures into the beginning of my romance. She was concerned that I'd make a mistake as I had before and flew to Los Angeles for dinner with Robert.
She's that kind of person. She and her husband Buddy Rhodes have been treasured friends over the years.

Niloufer Ichapora King not only has the sharpest palate known to man or woman, but knows how to listen and laugh in all the right places. When we have ailing birds, dogs or cats, we turn to one another.

Laurel Gonsalves believed in my writing before I did. She invited me on a trip to Oaxaca which turned into one of the first articles that *Saveur* magazine published. Her hospitality and New York savvy, love of the theater, art and good food opened my life to new possibilities. I'm grateful for her keen eye in reading and commenting on my work.

Thanks to Ingrid Kornspan, whose daughters, CoCo and LuLu are among my dearest friends. I hold their opinions in highest esteem. The laughs, the art and the naughty days keep me going in the driest of times.

I had a lot to be grateful to Linda and Rolando Klein for before Robert, but as a foursome, the friendship and support for each other has bloomed.

My gratitude to Eleanor Bertino for keeping me up on political details, the ins and outs of our common neighborhood, North Beach and for helping me in the beginning of my writing career. For someone who doesn't cook, she knows more about food than anyone.

My heartfelt love and thanks to Eleanor Coppola for her long friendship and for urging me to stretch outside the culinary world and to start this manuscript.

Eric Karpeles and Michael Sell always thought I was funnier than I knew. During early readings, they heard my voice in my written word. I could ask them and get honest answers if I ever appeared to brag or drop names. Beside extraordinary friendships, we shared some of the best meals in the past fifteen years.

And finally, I would dedicate this book to the late Mary Lloyd Estrin because I love and miss her so much, but since it's about falling in love with Robert, I'll leave it at that.

Robert & Peggy on their wedding day—February 13, 2009.

CPSIA information can be obtained
at www.ICGtesting.com
Printed in the USA
LVHW071752300621
691575LV00005B/242